CLAUDE AKE MEMORIAL PAPERS NO. 13

RESPONSES TO INSECURITY IN AFRICA : THE CHALLENGE OF PEACEBUILDING

By Kwesi Aning

UPPSALA
UNIVERSITET

**THE NORDIC
AFRICA INSTITUTE**
NORDISKA AFRIKAINSTITUTET

Indexing terms:

Africa
Peace
Peacebuilding
Regional security
Regionalism

Responses to Insecurity in Africa : The Challenge of Peacebuilding
Claude Ake Memorial Papers No 13

© 2024 Nordiska Afrikainstitutet/The Nordic Africa Institute, Institutionen för freds- och konfliktforskning
vid Uppsala universitet/University University Department of Peace and Conflict Research, and the author

Author: Kwesi Aning

ISSN 1654-7489
ISBN 978-91-7106-907-8   print-on-demand version
ISBN 978-91-7106-908-5   pdf e-book

Layout and Production Editor: Henrik Alfredsson
Front cover: Collage of the five photos from pages 4-5, 6, 12, 22 and 42.

The Nordic Africa Institute conducts independent, policy-relevant research, provides analysis and informs
decisionmaking, with the aim of advancing research-based knowledge of contemporary Africa. The institute is
jointly financed by the governments of Finland, Iceland and Sweden.

The opinions expressed in this volume are those of the author and do not necessarily reflect the views of the
Nordic Africa Institute.

CONTENTS

FOREWORD

A s a continent, Africa is central to world affairs. Yet it remains less well understood than it needs to be, if meaningful peace and development strategies are to be worked out. Indigenous scholarship is today contributing to provide this significant region with a voice of its own. The Claude Ake Visiting Chair – an initiative that began in 2003 – forms part of this effort. It remains a cooperative undertaking between the Department of Peace and Conflict Research at Uppsala University and the Nordic Africa Institute, also based in Uppsala, Sweden. It serves to honour the memory of Professor Claude Ake by offering a space for intellectuals involved in African affairs to pursue their academic interests. In this way, it seeks to promote deeper insights and wider perspectives for the benefit of African peace and development.

The initiative is a way to continue the efforts of Professor Claude Ake, who was a frequent visitor to Uppsala in the 1980s and 1990s. He was an extraordinarily talented researcher, with a commitment to justice, democracy and pan-Africanism. His untimely death in a plane crash in Nigeria in late 1996 came as a shock and was a major loss to the field of African affairs.

It fell to the two Uppsala institutions to raise the funds and initiate a visiting chair for scholars working on African affairs. The idea was to give the holder a semester in Uppsala, free from any tasks at home – enough time to pursue a research idea, complete an academic paper or initiate a new project. It has been possible to keep this effort going for over 20 years.

Bamako, Mali, March 2022. Photo: Mark Fischer.

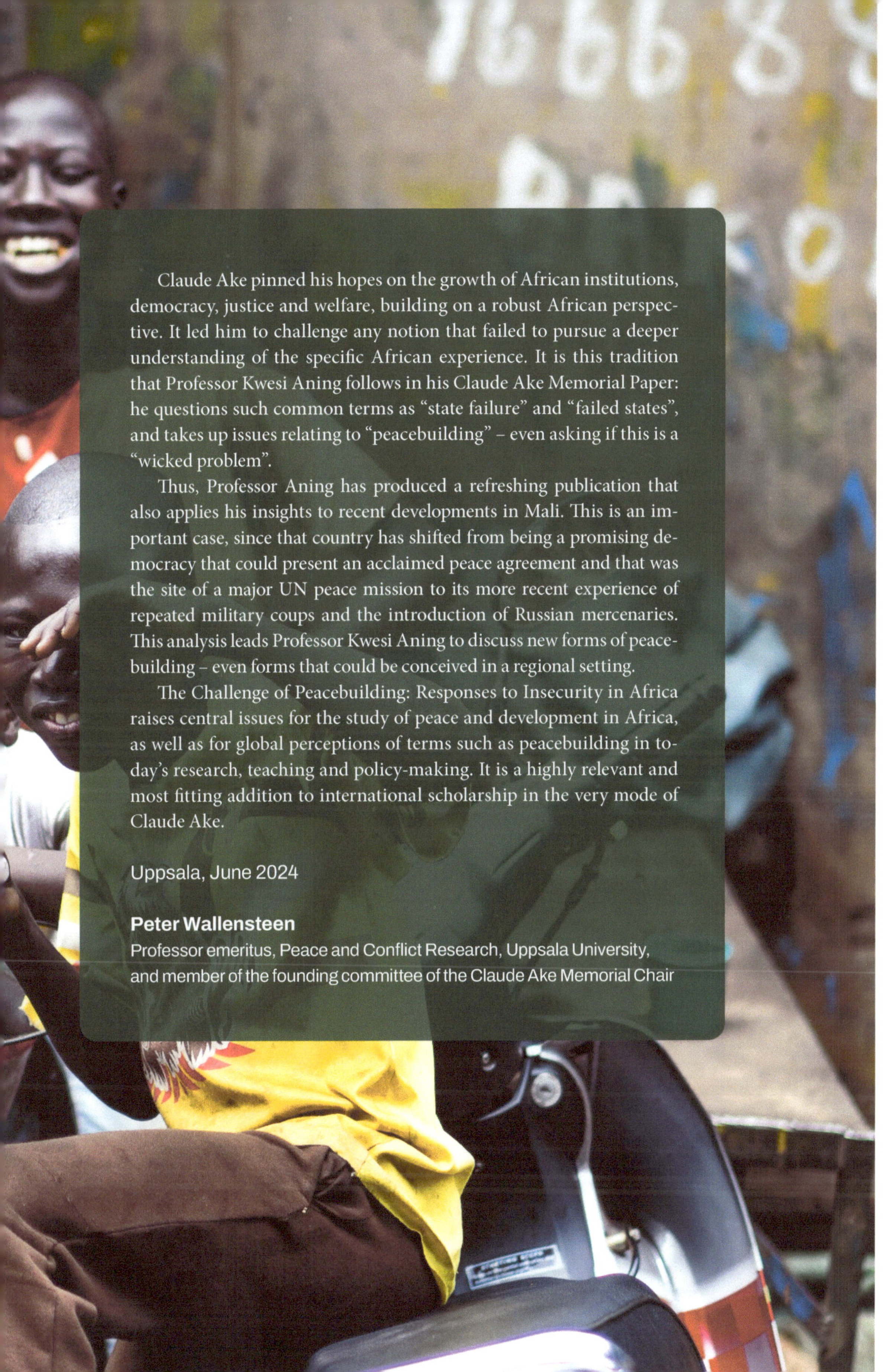

Claude Ake pinned his hopes on the growth of African institutions, democracy, justice and welfare, building on a robust African perspective. It led him to challenge any notion that failed to pursue a deeper understanding of the specific African experience. It is this tradition that Professor Kwesi Aning follows in his Claude Ake Memorial Paper: he questions such common terms as "state failure" and "failed states", and takes up issues relating to "peacebuilding" – even asking if this is a "wicked problem".

Thus, Professor Aning has produced a refreshing publication that also applies his insights to recent developments in Mali. This is an important case, since that country has shifted from being a promising democracy that could present an acclaimed peace agreement and that was the site of a major UN peace mission to its more recent experience of repeated military coups and the introduction of Russian mercenaries. This analysis leads Professor Kwesi Aning to discuss new forms of peacebuilding – even forms that could be conceived in a regional setting.

The Challenge of Peacebuilding: Responses to Insecurity in Africa raises central issues for the study of peace and development in Africa, as well as for global perceptions of terms such as peacebuilding in today's research, teaching and policy-making. It is a highly relevant and most fitting addition to international scholarship in the very mode of Claude Ake.

Uppsala, June 2024

Peter Wallensteen
Professor emeritus, Peace and Conflict Research, Uppsala University, and member of the founding committee of the Claude Ake Memorial Chair

The gatekeepers of the garden must necessarily perform their duties by taking care not only 'of the garden itself, but [of] the jungle outside'.

Page 10

INTRODUCTION

Since its introduction by former UN Secretary-General Boutros Boutros-Ghali in the *Agenda for Peace* in 1992, the concept of peacebuilding has become a critical component of international intervention schemes to prevent conflict and rebuild states. Subsequently, it has spawned a variety of conceptual ideas that seek to grasp *what* it is and *how* the concept should be understood and applied in practice. For the purposes of this paper, the wide-ranging outcomes of such deliberations raise several questions about how the discourse surrounding threats is constructed – and, more fundamentally, what the concept and practice of peacebuilding is good for. How have the conceptualisations, prevalent discursive dichotomies and subsequent practical applications of the concept contributed to dealing with and providing solutions to the myriad insecurities on the African continent? The 1992 UN document characterised peacebuilding as 'actions to identify and support structures which will tend to solidify peace to avoid a relapse into conflict'.[1] Since its early days,[2] the concept has embodied a significant degree of conceptual muddle and theoretical disagreement. As a result, Carey and Sen[3] lament the conceptual fuzziness and seek to 'bridge what appear to be six or seven paradigmatic differences founded on different assumptions, questions, and conclusions about what is significant about the peacebuilding efforts' that have been undertaken since 1992.[4] While they argue that 'policy makers and practitioners may not ordinarily benefit from theoretical debates among academics',[5] in this paper I will argue the reverse: that such debates impact on policy processes leading to how insecurities are constructed and responded to. Such debates span the scope of challenges faced by states experiencing 'conflict, fragility, and crisis on the one hand, and poverty and inequality on the other'. These, according to McCandless intertwine 'in catastrophic and morally unacceptable ways, demanding integrated, concerted attention'.[6]

---

1   UN 1992.
2   A good overview of the literature dealing with the historical developments of the concept are Johan Galtung, 1976. 'Three Approaches to Peace: Peacekeeping, peacemaking and peacebuilding', in Johan Galtung, Ed., Peace, War and Defence: Essays in Peace Research (Copenhagen: Christian Ejlers); Michael Barnett, et al., 2007. 'Peacebuilding: What is in a name?', Global Governance, 13 (1), pp. 35-58; Lederach, John Paul. 2012. 'The origins and evolution of infrastructures for peace', Journal of Peacebuilding and Development, 7 (3).
3   Carey, Henry F. and Onur Sen.2019. 'Bridging the Conceptual and Theoretical Divides on Peace and Peacebuilding', p. 1 in Carey, H. (Ed.). (2020). Peacebuilding Paradigms: The Impact of Theoretical Diversity on Implementing Sustainable Peace. Cambridge: Cambridge University Press.
4   Ibid.
5   Ibid, p. 1.
6   McCandless, E. (2021). Critical Evolutions in the Peacebuilding-Development Praxis Nexus: Crisis and Complexity, Synergy and Transformation. Journal of Peacebuilding & Development, 16(2), p.133; McCandless, E. 2019. Beyond Liberal and Local Peacebuilding Three Critical Framings to Approach the Complexity of Conflict and Fragility in Africa, Africa Insight, 49, (3), p. 21.

Since the 1960s, security-focused research on sub-Saharan Africa has expanded in part due to a recognition that this is the most vulnerable continent. The argument is that African insecurities and vulnerabilities could spread to far-off regions. This has resulted both in a discourse and praxis that demonstrate how historical and structural forces locate Africa at the centre of all manner of exploratory intervention practices. Since the 1960s alone, close to 50 peace operations have been deployed on the continent. Yet, these missions – which have seen a growth in troop numbers, scale and cost of operations alike – have resulted in two mutually reinforcing dynamics: (a) an increase in the number of missions by African regional organisations and troop and police contributing countries (T/PCCs); and (b) an increase in the number of missions that are largely funded by Africa's external partners.[7] In spite of the rise in the number of missions and in the financial outlay, the proliferation of regional and international approaches and measures that seek to alleviate insecurity in the Sahel (comprising Mali, Burkina Faso and Niger), for example, and to build the capacities of actors (especially among statutory security forces) has led to a sense of 'permanency',[8] and has resulted in a 'security traffic jam'[9] – even though the interventions have not by themselves brought any demonstrably marked improvement to Mali's security conundrum.[10] As will be shown later, the narratives leading to Mali being the destination of choice for security actors provide justification for, first the selection and then discourses that created an acceptability for an eventual international intervention. In Mali's case, it was not only the humanitarian situation that stimulated the international response. Rather, two factors were at play in making the country an irresistible target for international attention. First, there is the presence of al-Qaeda in the Islamic Maghreb (AQIM): the name alone was enough to distort policy approaches and recommendations and to place Mali

---

7   Aubyn, F. et al., 2019. 'UN Funding Cuts for Peacekeeping have Consequences for Ghana: After Sixty years of UN Peacekeeping' DIIS Policy Brief, https://www.diis.dk/en/research/un-funding-cuts-peacekeeping-consequences-ghana; Williams, P. 2021. 'Learning lessons from peace operations in Africa', in McNamee, T and M. Muyangwa (Eds.), The State of Peacebuilding in Africa: Lessons Learned for Policymakers and Practitioners, (Cham: Palgrave Macmillan), pp. 15-32; The top 10 providers of assessed contributions to United Nations peacekeeping operations for 2020-2021 are: United States (27.89%); China (15.21%); Japan (8.56%); Germany (6.09%); United Kingdom (5.79%); France (5.61%); Italy (3.30%); Russian Federation (3.04%); Canada (2.73%); Republic of Korea (2.26%). For the complete list of assessed contributions by country, 2019-2021, see A/73/350/Add.1 How we are funded | United Nations Peacekeeping

8   Tull, D.M. 2019. 'Rebuilding Mali's army: the dissonant relationship between Mali and its international partners', International Affairs 95 (2) pp. 405–22. Tull posits that, the Malian army was an entity in a permanent state of being 'capacity-built'.

9   Cold-Ravnkilde, S. M. and Katja Lindskov Jacobsen, 2020. 'Disentangling the security traffic jam in the Sahel: constitutive effects of contemporary interventionism', International Affairs 96 (4), 2020, p. 857

10   UN Secretary-General's reports on Mali, present a dire picture in which the situation has steadily deteriorated since 2015. 'The security situation in the Sahel subregion continued to deteriorate.' See UNSC, Situation in Mali: report of the Secretary-General, UN Doc. S/2021/519 (New York, 1 June 2021)

firmly on the front line of the global war on terror.[11] Second, there is the lack of appetite among the world's major powers for sending their own soldiers into battle in strange, foreign lands.[12]

Such endeavours by international actors 'often emphasise synergies between what are commonly framed as multidimensional and comprehensive approaches, aimed in most cases at rebuilding "failed" states and often times at stabilising the entire region'[13]. These have contributed to creating operational environments characterised by 'differences and disagreements' and a diversity of 'unsynchronised intervention actors'.[14] Other commentators argue that these 'actors' must be seen as part of 'a governance apparatus', whose 'practices constitute counter-insurgency governance: a set of power relations and configurations that emphasise the "terrorist threat" and *enact the conditions for perpetual intervention'.*[15] It is argued that the intervention was:

> imperfectly coordinated, incomplete and in flux. [Such intervention] reacts and adapts to local acts of disturbance or resistance (such as jihadist attacks and expansion, or coups d'état). Its agendas and policies can collide in attempts at managing the conflicts. Yet, ultimately, many actors and activities converge in the construction of an emerging regional security governance structure.[16]

Creating the prerequisites and discourses around which particular states can be constructed as 'failed', 'failing' and 'collapsed' states produces the conditions that enables external actors to 'enact and sustain an international politics of permanent

11   Aning, Kwesi. 2010. 'Security, war on terror and ODA', Critical Studies on Terrorism, 3 (2) pp. 7-26.

12   Alison, Simon. 2012.'Military intervention in Mali: a dangerous idea with too much support', at https://www.theguardian.com/world/2012/oct/17/military-intervention-mali-dangerous-idea accessed 10 October 2022; Aubyn, F, et al., 2019. 'UN Funding Cuts for Peacekeeping have Consequences for Ghana: After Sixty years of UN Peacekeeping' DIIS Policy Brief UN funding cuts for peacekeeping have consequences for Ghana | DIIS; Contribution of Uniformed Personnel to UN by Country and Personnel Type, Experts on Mission, Formed Police Units, Individual Police, Staff Officer, and Troops As of : 30/09/2022 at https://peacekeeping.un.org/sites/default/files/01_contributions_to_un_peacekeeping_operations_by_country_and_post_54_september_22.pdf . Of the top 21 T/PCCs Africa was in 15 of these positions.

13   Cold-Ravnkilde and Jacobsen, op cit.,

14   Cold-Ravnkilde and Jacobsen, ibid

15   Charbonneau, B. 2021. 'Counter-insurgency governance in the Sahel', International Affairs, 97 (6), p. 1816. See for example, Grovogui, Siba. N. (2002). Regimes of Sovereignty: International Morality and the African Condition. European Journal of International Relations, 8(3), 315–338.

16   Charbonneau provides a compelling argument about how notions of African politics and realities have contributed to situations where, '...Westphalian commonsense and its model of statehood are not attuned to the circumstances upon which they are made to bear', p.335

intervention – of reframing security and development policies in terms of indefinitely managing or responding to future … risks and conflicts in the Sahel so that they do not threaten the status quo'.[17] However, Susan Woodward has argued that such classification 'is a political threat to countries so labelled'.[18] By establishing a narrative of failure, a situation is created in which the predominant understanding of conflict (and its corollary – insecurity) – especially in the post-Cold War era – demonstrates the political nature of these interpretations. Such discourses, which sometimes permeate policy spaces, were best captured in the words of Josep Borrell, the EU's foreign policy head, who divided the world into 'gardens' and 'jungles', and cautioned about the need for 'more engage[ment] with the rest of the world'. Failure to act pre-emptively will end in the 'the rest of the world invad[ing] us'.[19] This discursive practice of framing African insecurities and their potential to 'invade' the garden means that the gatekeepers of the garden must necessarily perform their duties by taking care not only 'of the garden itself, but [of] the jungle outside'.[20] Wai denotes such processes of framing as the internalisation of the causes of conflicts: he defines internalisation as 'the move to locate the causes of conflicts in internal *sources*. It is the assumption that the causes of conflicts are *endogenously located in local conditions bound to what is seen as the internal dysfunctions of these societies*.'[21] Interpretation then becomes an important aspect and component of how such conflicts are understood and responded to in an effort to resolve them. However, interpretations are not wholly neutral or devoid of bias on the part of the interpreter. Thus, constructing a situation in which:

> the act of interpretation is thus not only harmful for what counts and how it is constructed, but also for what does not count, for everything that omits and does not give voice (the silences), as well as for its inability or unwillingness to incorporate voices from different worldviews that question the dominant thinking.[22]

---

17 Charbonneau, B. 2022. 'The climate of counterinsurgency and the future of security in the Sahel', *Environmental Science and Policy*, p. 138.

18 Woodward, S.L. 2017. *The Ideology of Failed States. Why Intervention Fails* Cambridge: Cambridge University Press.

19 'European Diplomatic Academy: Opening remarks by High Representative Josep Borrell at the inauguration of the pilot programme', 13 Oct. 2022, https://www.eeas.europa.eu/eeas/european-diplomatic-academy-opening-remarks-high-representative-josep-borrell-inauguration_en. See also, Vijay Prashad. 2022. *Africa Does Not Want to Be a Breeding Ground for the New Cold War:* The Forty-Fourth Newsletter. For a subsequent clarification, see, https://www.eeas.europa.eu/eeas/metaphors-and-geo-politics_en

20 Ibid.

21 Wai, Zubairu. 2022. 'About a Will to Power: Post-cold War Conflicts and the Politics of Knowledge Production', *Tripodos*, number 51, p.34 (my emphasis).

22 Mateos, Òscar, & Rodríguez, A. I. 2022. Understanding Peace, Conflict and Security Through Alternative Narratives. *Tripodos*, (51), p.9

From the above, it becomes obvious and apparent that, '[i]n a world of no easy decisions and perhaps only difficult and impossible choices', the need 'to practice ethics – ethical reflexivity' and to add positionality becomes critical. Even such criticality, in the words of Ba, may still exhibit signs of 'fissures, slippages and inconsistencies between … thought and action'. The analytical utility of such endeavours is, as Ba argues, that 'at the very least, [it] highlight[s] [their limitations]'.[23]

This paper undertakes a critical interrogation, highlighting the way in which knowledge about *peacebuilding* is generated and how that contributes to *dominant interpretations* of its application and practice in the Sahel. I begin by discussing: (a) the nexus between peacebuilding and post-colonial knowledge generation; (b) the extent to which such discursive narratives turn peacebuilding into a wicked problem (and what can and must be done about that); (c) how a move to come to terms with the regional interconnectedness of seemingly domestic insecurities through a regional peacebuilding lens can create better options to appreciate the networked and intertwined nature of insecurity; (d) how hybrid forms of peacebuilding contributes to the construction governance processes that are context-specific; and (e) how these ideas contributed to the discursive construction of insecurity in Mali, which eventually resulted in stalemate in the country and made the peacebuilding interventions difficult to implement. The paper argues that an awareness of positionality and reflexivity provides opportunities for more nuanced hybrid security and political orders during peacebuilding endeavours. Finally, I offer some concluding thoughts.

---

23   Ba, Oumar. 2022. 'The Europeans and Americans Don't Know Africa': Of Translation, Interpretation, and Extraction', Millennium- Journal of International Studies, 50 (2), January, p.550; Jeremiah O. Arowosegbe. 2011. State reconstruction in Africa: the relevance of Claude Ake's political thought', International Affairs, 87 (3), May, pages 651-670

The hegemonic structuring of knowledge generation and its attendant distribution exemplify the hierarchies of power, constitutive of the Western mode of organising science.

Page 15

Porto-Novo, Benin, May 2022. Mariam Chabi Talata, vice president of Benin, receives Assimi Goita, coup leader and interim president of Mali. Photo: Official Office of the President of Benin.

AKE, POST-COLONIAL KNOWLEDGE GENERATION AND PEACEBUILDING

In a lecture dedicated to Claude Ake, one needs to raise the fundamental question of the extent to which Ake's works are relevant to the topic under discussion. Ake's thoughts on the state, social sciences and knowledge generation, endogenous forms of statehood, development, politics, violence and reconstruction are all germane aspects of the complexity of the issues that peacebuilding seeks to tackle. This is succinctly captured by Tschirgi, who follows (indirectly) in Ake's footsteps to link peacebuilding to questions of security and development. When peacebuilding is linked to security and development, the three elements 'offer an integrated approach to understanding and dealing with the full range of issues that threatened peace and security'.[24]

International peacebuilding operations typically seek to prevent conflict recurrence in countries that are making the transition from civil war to lasting peace;[25] but they often come with other, less-explicit objectives. As Roland Paris argues, 'peacebuilding missions are not merely exercises in conflict management'.[26] Prominent among the less obvious agendas has been the instrumentalisation of peace missions as mechanisms for disseminating different norms and values to so-called 'failing', 'failed' or 'fragile' states in the ongoing contexts of globalisation and the 'global war on terror'.[27] The transference of these norms and values – which are obviously embodied in the idea of the liberal peace – is invariably accompanied by

---

24 Tschirgi, N. 2003. Peacebuilding as the Link between Security and Development: Is the Window of Opportunity Closing? (New York: International Peace Academy), p. 1

25 Kofi Annan, 'The Causes of Conflict and the Promotion of Durable Peace and Sustainable Development in Africa', Report of the Secretary-General to the Security Council, S/l998/318 (13 April, 1998), para. 63; Doyle, Michael W. and Nicholas Sambanis, 'International Peacebuilding: A Theoretical and Quantitative Analysis', American Political Science Review 94 (4), 2000, pp. 779-801; Aning, Kwesi. 2005. "The Challenges to Multilateral Interventions - UN, ECOWAS and Complex Political Emergencies in West Africa: A Critical Analysis', Journal of Asian & African Studies, 4, (1- 2); See Adetula, V., Bereketeab, R., & Obi, C. (Eds.,).2020. Regional Economic Communities and Peacebuilding in Africa: Lessons from ECOWAS and IGAD (1st ed.). Routledge, p. 7 for a discussion of the 1995 Supplement to the Agenda for Peace and the subsequent Brahimi Report. The 2007 UNSG Policy Committee characterised peacebuilding as, 'a range of measures targeted to reduce the risk of lapsing or relapsing into conflict by strengthening national capacities at all levels for conflict management and to lay the foundations for a sustainable peace and development'.

26 Paris, R 2002. 'International peacebuilding and the 'mission civilisatrice', Review of International Studies 28, p. 638.

27 Newman, E. 2011. 'A human security peace-building agenda', Third World Quarterly 32, (10), pp 1737–1756; Aning, Kwesi. 2010. 'Security, war on terror and ODA', Critical Studies on Terrorism', 3 (2), pp. 7-26.

a mode of discursive constructions that recycles colonial-era assumptions,[28] in order to structure and reproduce responses to humanitarian crises in African spaces along the lines of a 'victim–rescuer model'.[29] Such an approach – seeking as it does to invent an African absence by mainstream security and peacebuilding scholarship – is intended to diminish African agency, in order to justify the perpetuation of Western paternalism on the continent.[30] In effect, mainstream scholarship has tended to transform people and social groups in Africa into objects (that need to be secured), rather than subjects of security (with agency). Such an approach signifies 'epistemic injustice',[31] resulting in what Òscar Mateos and Ana Isabel Rodríguez characterise as 'epistemic violence' or 'epistemicide',[32] understood as an attempt to discover just what happens to the very different worldview and to the political and social consequences of the ideological imperialism manifest in editorial decisions about what counts as 'knowledge'. It highlights the problematic nature of this approach and its inadequacy to explain reality to us.

The absence fallacy is also deployed to deny the existence of African history and African knowledge. At best, knowledge generated from African sources is downgraded to the status of myths, folklore or opinions that serve as a foil to European superiority in knowledge generation.[33] This Eurocentric monopoly of knowledge generation and its eventual distribution leads to scientific 'epistemicide' and results in 'continued exclusionary knowledge production practices'.[34] A marked feature of this epistemological hegemony is the division of labour, in which researchers/scholars from the global North serve as teachers and rule-setters/enforcers, while their Southern counterparts on the receiving end of this unequal power relationship are consigned to the position of learners and rule-takers.[35] As is argued elsewhere:

---

28   Falola, T. 1988 Decolonizing African Studies: knowledge production, agency, and Voice (Rochester, NY: University of Rochester Press); V-Y Mudimbe, The Invention of Africa, (Bloomington, IN: Indiana University Press).

29   Pugh, Michael. 2004. 'Peacekeeping and critical theory', International Peacekeeping 11 (1), p. 48.

30   See for example, Archaya, Amitav, Paul Henri-Bischoff, Kwesi Aning, 2015. 'Africa in global international relations: emerging approaches to theory and practice – an introduction' in Amitav Archaya, Paul Henri-Bischoff, Kwesi Aning, Eds., Africa in Global International Relations: emerging approaches to theory and practice (London: Routledge)

31   Johnson, A. K., Lechartre, J., Mart, Ş. G., Robison, M. D., & Hughes, C. (2022). Peace scholarship and the local turn: Hierarchies in the production of knowledge about peace. Journal of Peace Research, 0(0), p.2.

32   Mateos and Rodriguez, op cit; See also, Bennett, Karen. 2007. 'Epistemicide! The Tale of a Predatory Discourse, November, Translator 13(2):151-169.

33   Chinweizu Ibekwe, Decolonising the African mind (Lagos: Sundoor, 1987); Ngũgĩ wa Thiong'o, Decolonising the mind: the politics of language in African literature (London and Portsmouth, NH: James Currey and Heinemann, 1986); Hugh Trevor-Roper, The rise of Christian Europe (London: Thames & Hudson, 1966); Finn Fuglestad, 'The Trevor-Roper trap or the imperialism of history: an essay', History in Africa, vol. 19, 1992, pp. 309–26.

34   Johnson, A. K., et al. (2022 p. 13.

35   Aning, Kwesi et al. 'Decolonising Academic Collaboration: South-North Perspectives', DIIS Policy Brief, May 2022 https://pure.diis.dk/ws/files/5428162/DIIS_PB_Decolonising_Academic_Collaboration.pdf

> Structural biases in academia are the product of lopsided power relations. They have historical roots in colonial legacies but are perpetuated by contemporary dynamics of inequalities between South and North. Financial support for research projects usually comes from donor agencies in the North. Consequently, it is often Northern research institutions that define the focus of research and set the agenda on which methodological and theoretical approaches to apply.[36]

Such modes of knowledge generation, distribution and consumption enable Western academics to arrogate to themselves the role of knowledge producers, while African scholars are relegated to the position of knowledge consumers, leading to a Western (re)engineering of transitional societies along the lines of liberal peace assumptions.[37] In other words, social location or positionality determines epistemic location within a global scheme, in which this inequality in knowledge production affects both the *idea* and the *implementation* of peace missions. The end result is that

> there is a significant risk that the production of knowledge does not reflect the needs, interests and perspectives of academics and stakeholders in African countries. Research results may furthermore be irrelevant or miss vital points because the framing, methodologies, and analysis of research projects and findings overlook key aspects of the local context and people's lived experiences.[38]

The hegemonic structuring of knowledge generation and its attendant distribution exemplify the hierarchies of power, constitutive of the Western mode of organising science, and deny peace and security research the opportunity to understand effectively the insecurities in African locales and the kind of frameworks that could serve to bolster the resilience of states and societies on the continent. Such approaches generate counterproductive policy outcomes in many instances – as the case of the Sahel (particularly Mali discussed below) shows. The multiple and complex nature of insecurities in Africa and the multiplicity of state and non-state actors that deliver

---

36   Ibid., p. 2.
37   Richmond, O.P. 2008. Peace in International Relations (London: Routledge); Johnson, et. al., op cit., p. 3ff.
38   Aning, et. al., p. 2.

political and security governance on the continent suggest a need to rethink concepts and approaches, so that they transcend the traditional statist diplomacy and include resources and capacities at different sites and scales of society that support peace-building from within.[39] This is because the state in Africa is fundamentally different from the Weberian model[40] and is 'embedded in [multiple] entities, including society',[41] rendering the statist assumptions of International Relations (IR) theory and liberal peace approaches reductionist. Moreover, in the African context – where the state itself continues to serve as a major source of insecurity for individuals and groups – a critical reflection on the role played by diverse peacebuilders (including those operating outside the realm of the legally constituted state) seems inevitable. However, mainstream scholarship hinders systematic inquiry into these realities – a point eloquently made by Cooper, who argues that the price of the continual misrepresentation of events in Africa as 'a lack, a failure or distortion' is that 'one fails to ask what is actually happening in Africa'.[42] Others have taken up this mode of analysis and pathological interpretations, arguing that 'political orders in Africa, ... are not judged by what they are, but by what they are not'[43]. Rather, there is a need to 'engage with alternative systems of order which have often been more successful than formal governance arrangements in the crumbling institutional environments of contemporary Africa'.[44] Such explanatory analytical frameworks of African politics draw heavily on analogies with Western experiences, disguised as universal experiences, and on what Mamdani calls 'history by analogy'.[45] Osaghae, for example, argues that:

> The main concern of analogical analysis is not however to mainstream African formations as historical latecomers in a world history that assumes convergence in supposedly universal categories, but to exceptionalize them as deviant cases. The flaw in this form of analysis is the tendency to underplay or peripheralize

39   Ake, C. 1993. 'The Unique Case of African Democracy', International Affairs 69 (2), pp. 239–244; Richmond, O.P. 2013. 'Peace formation and local infrastructures for peace', Alternatives: Global, Local, Political, 38 (4), pp. 271-287; Lederach, op cit., pp. 8-13.
40   Aubyn, F and Kwesi Aning. 2018. 'Challenging conventional understandings of statehood based on West African Realities' in Kwesi Aning, M. Anne Brown, Volker Boege & Charles T. Hunt. (Eds.), Exploring Peace formations: justice and security in post-conflict states. (London: Routledge) pp.24-38
41   Tieku, Thomas Kwasi, 2021. 'The Legon School of International Relations', Review of International Studies, 47(5) pp. 656-671.
42   Cooper, Frederick. 2001. 'What Is the Concept of Globalization Good for? An African Historian's Perspective', African Affairs, vol. 100, no. 399, pp. 189–213.
43   Ibid
44   Meagher, K. (2012), The Strength of Weak States? Non-State Security Forces and Hybrid Governance in Africa. Development and Change, 43, p. 1074.
45   Mamdani, M. 1996. Citizen and Subject: Contemporary Africa and the Legacy of Late Colonialism (Princeton: Princeton University Press), p. 9.

> the history of the analogous or deviant case, which is assumed to lack both original history and an authentic future.[46]

These analyses, in the words of Mamdani, are not based on a factual assessment of the object in question; namely Africa. They are based on an assessment 'not in terms of what it was, but with reference to what it was not'[47]. To circumvent such weaknesses, Olonisakin and colleagues argue that peacebuilding, for example, 'should be conceived as part of the conversations occurring in the continuum of statebuilding in the affected societies'.[48] They introduce the notion of *conversations*, and argue that much of the conflicts in Africa occurs as a consequence of the complexity of such conversations, which take place at various national levels and in various contexts – 'initially between colonial elites and African peoples and societies; and in the post-independence period, between governing elites and their people'[49]. But this argument can and should be pushed further. I argue that the conversations should take place between different elite factions and among the different diverse populations of a state. As a result, they argue that when conflicts occur, escalate and become intractable, *'peace-building interventions would do well to return to the conversations that led to violence in the first place'* (my emphasis).[50] The argument here is that any attempt at peacebuilding must seek a return to the series of conversations that led to the misunderstandings and unresolved contentions which generated and contributed to the initial disagreements about the state-building and national integration project. When one follows this line of argument, then the logical flow is that one can extend such analysis to the construction of security and insecurity, and by inference to how peacebuilding should be constructed and practised as a response. Newman argues that:

> The use of the failed state label – when it is applied, why, and with what effect – and the perception of threats inherent in conflict-prone societies are not a reflection of objective truth or reality, but of a subjective interpretation of events. As a demonstration

---

46   See Osaghae, E.E. 2006. Colonialism and Civil Society in Africa: The Perspective of Ekeh's Two Publics. Voluntas 17, 233–245.

47   Mamdani, op cit.,

48   Olonisakin, Funmi, Alagaw Ababu Kifle & Alfred Muteru (2021) Introduction: reframing narratives of peace-building and state-building in Africa, Conflict, Security & Development, 21 (4), pp.401ff.

49   Ibid.

50   Ibid, p. 402. Furthermore, they argue that, such conversations need not be 'not restricted to structured, overt, and delineated verbal dialogues, discussions, or exchanges that occur between a variety of actors within society. Rather, we are particularly interested in the wider-ranging interactions among groups in society – however unstructured, unseen, inexplicit, and violent the conversations are – and their resulting signifiers'.

> of the importance of political constructions, the empirical reality of failed states is in many ways actually less important than the perception of powerful actors towards the concept and the security threats inherent in them. Viewing peacebuilding as a part of the 'security' agenda is therefore a part of the process by which threats and challenges are constructed and responded to.[51]

This is partly a reflection of the persistent dominance of the modernisation paradigm, which posits the West as the fulcrum of world history and development.[52] However, after a period of multiple crises and critical readings,[53] the theory and practice of international peacebuilding appear to be moving away from liberal forms of intervention, giving policy frameworks a positive and renewed impetus. Similar to today's multilateral agendas for sustaining development and security,[54] international involvements in conflict-affected countries seem to require a prolonged and continued engagement.[55] For example, in 2016, the twin resolutions of the General Assembly (70/262) and the Security Council (2282) emphasised the need to 'work together to sustain peace at all stages of conflict and in all its dimensions', and 'not only once conflict had broken out but also long beforehand, through the prevention of conflict and addressing its root causes'.[56]

Pol Bargués, for example, discusses how the understanding of risks threatens initiatives: 'the risks of increasing tensions and causing damage', 'the risk of failure, the risk of inefficiency, the risk of diversion of funds' and many more.[57] While risks cannot be prevented, international stakeholders are expected to learn from experience, be modest and reflective, and develop flexible programmes for disas-

---

51 Simon Alison. 2012.'Military intervention in Mali: a dangerous idea with too much support', at www.theguardian.com/world/2012/oct/17/military-intervention-mali-dangerous-idea assessed 10 October 2022. Alison argues that, '...[to] be honest: it's not the humanitarian situation that is animating the international response, 17 October; Newman, Edward. 2010. 'Peacebuilding as Security in 'Failing' and Conflict Prone States', Journal of Intervention and Statebuilding, 4 (30, 305-322.

52 See Osaghae, op cit,. Mamdani, 1996, p. 9. See, also, Peter P. Ekeh. 1975. "Colonialism and the Two Publics in Africa: A Theoretical Statement," Comparative Studies in Society and History, 17 (1)

53 Nadarajah, Suthaharan and Rampton, David, 2015. 'The limits of hybridity and the crisis of liberal peace', Review of International Studies, 41 (1) pp. 49–72

54 UN, 'Transforming our World: the 2030 Agenda for Sustainable Development' (General Assembly, 2015).

55 UN, 'The Challenge of Sustaining Peace: Report of the Advisory Group of Experts for the 2015 Review of the United Nations Peacebuilding Architecture' (New York: United Nations, 2015), pp. 7, 8, 18.

56 UN, 'Peacebuilding and Sustaining Peace: Report of the Secretary-General' (General Assembly and Security Council, 2018), p. 1.

57 Bargués, Pol. 2020. 'Peacebuilding without peace? On how pragmatism complicates the practice of international intervention', Review of International Studies, 46 2); Aoi, Chiyuki, De Coning, Cedric, and Thakur, Ramesh Chandra, 2007. Unintended Consequences of Peacekeeping Operations (Tokyo and New York: United Nations University Press)

ter preparedness and resilience.[58] In spite of the risks, the 1990s not only saw an increase in UN peacekeeping missions, but also a steady expansion of the ambitious goals they were created to achieve,[59] including the rise in peacebuilding activities that have resulted in 'an elaborate institutional architecture at the global and regional level', but little or no effort to examine 'the highly problematic consequences of contemporary peacebuilding practices'.[60] As a result, Omeje argues that peacebuilding must progress beyond the 'menace' of impending risks to serve the 'legitimate interests and well-being' of the broadest base of [Africa's] peoples'.[61] Consequently, peacebuilding scholars have started to explain the poor record of international interventions by highlighting the insufficient or limited attempts at engaging more fully and genuinely with the differences in the processes of peacebuilding.[62]

According to the UN Secretary-General's 2018 report on peacebuilding and sustaining peace, '[a]n ecosystem of partners ... is critical to sustaining peace'.[63] It is this ability (or lack thereof) of those on the security and development side of this peacebuilding ecosystem to build partnerships that has become more of a challenge than those in whose name they come as beneficiaries. Rather, peacebuilding must seek to understand their potential contribution 'as being in dialogue with the array of prevailing socio-cultural, political and historical conditions'.[64] According to Terence McNamee and Monde Muyangwa:

---

58   Dalgaard-Nielsen, Anja. 2017. Organizational resilience in national security bureaucracies: Realistic and practicable? Journal of Contingencies and Crises Management, 25 (4), December, pp. 341-349; Andersen, Ben. 2015. What Kind of Thing is Resilience? Politics, 35 (1), argues that, '...Resilience is described in different ways and as different kinds of things. Resilience is characterized as: 'ethos', 'programme', 'ideology', 'concept', 'term', 'governing rationality', 'doctrine', 'discourse', 'epistemic field', 'logic', 'buzzword', 'normative or ideal concept', 'strategy of power'. 'While not completely separate, these are not the same kinds of things', pp. 60-66

59   Aning, Kwesi, Fiifi Edu-Afful, 2016. 'African Agency in R2P: Interventions by African Union and ECOWAS in Mali, Cote D'ivoire, and Libya', International Studies Review, 18 (1), March, pp. 120–133.

60   Zaum, Dominik, 2011. 'Review essay; beyond the "Liberal Peace', Global Governance: A Review of Multilateralism and International Organizations, 18 (1), pp. 121-132.

61   Omeje, K., (ed.), 2018. 'Introduction'. In Peacebuilding in Contemporary Africa: In Search of Alternative Strategies. London, New York: Routledge, 3–19. Some elements and core themes of peacebuilding include among others: conflict prevention and early warning systems; mediation and conflict management; post-conflict reconstruction; disarmament, demobilisation, and reintegration (DDR); human rights and justice; and the role of women, religion, humanitarianism, grassroots organisations, and regional and continental bodies.

62   Bargués-Pedreny, Pol & Xavier Mathieu 2018. Beyond Silence, Obstacle and Stigma: Revisiting the 'Problem' of Difference in Peacebuilding, Journal of Intervention and Statebuilding, 12 (3), pp. 283-299.

63   UN General Assembly and Security Council, Peacebuilding and Sustaining Peace—Report of the Secretary-General, UN Doc. A/72/707–S/2018/43, January 18, 2018; Lara, Christian and Bariel Delsol. 2020. Sustaining Peace in Burkina Faso: Responding to an Emerging Crisis. International Peace Institute, May

64   Aning and Brown, 'Introduction'

> The concept of 'peacebuilding' has been, to say the least, variously defined. For some, it is one of several distinct activities including: conflict prevention and mediation (e.g., early warning and urgent diplomatic measures); peacemaking (e.g., high-level envoys and summits); peace enforcement (e.g., violent and non-violent coercive measures), and post-conflict reconstruction (including justice, institution-building, and economic development). All of which, in their own way, contribute to international peace and security. And then there are peacekeepers, who are increasingly mandated – or at least find themselves working – across different realms: protecting civilians, delivering humanitarian assistance, helping to restore the rule of law, even engaging in de facto reconstruction and state-building. Others use the term 'peacebuilding' in an instrumental sense: the means to institutionalize peace, and remove the root causes of conflict.[65]

Furthermore, there are concerns about the undue actions of interveners who tend to overly 'romanticise'[66] or 'sanitise'[67] the local. This is a point expanded further by Forsyth and colleagues, who argue against 'romanticising and homogenising' the complexity of existing power differentials, as they can disguise fundamental inequalities.[68] A corollary to this process of romanticisation is the 'de-mystif[ication of] the international',[69] in which those who are favoured or elevated may not always be the most appropriate representatives of their communities,[70] but rather a 'social engineering [of] the local for peace',[71] whereby international actors selectively choose those to partner with that distorts traditional and socially accepted power hierarchies. Such literature underscores how peacebuilding actors tend to ignore their own role in discursively constructing the 'local', thereby obscuring the politi-

65 2021. The State of Peacebuilding in Africa: Lessons Learned for Policymakers and Practitioners. (Cham: Palgrave Macmillan), p.6 it can also be read at https://link.springer.com/content/pdf/10.1007/978-3-030-46636-7.pdf

66 Richmond, O. 2009. 'The Romanticisation of the Local: Welfare, Culture and Peacebuilding', The International Spectator, 44 (1) pp.149ff March.;

67 Hudson, Heidi. 2016. 'Decolonising gender and peacebuilding: feminist frontiers and border thinking in Africa', Peacebuilding 4 (2), pp.194ff.

68 Forsyth, Miranda. et al. 2017. 'Hybridity in peacebuilding and development: a critical approach', Third World Thematics, 2 (4), p.410

69 Richmond, O.P. 2011 De-romanticizing the local, de-mystifying the international: hybridity in Timor Leste and the Solomon Islands, The Pacific Review, 24 (1) pp. 115-136.

70 Paffenholz, Thania. 2015. 'Unpacking the Local Turn in Peacebuilding: a critical assessment towards an agenda for future research'. Third World Quarterly 36 (5) pp.857-874.

71 Birgit Brauchler. 2017. 'Social engineering the local for peace', Social Anthropology, 25 (4), p. 437-453.

cal choices they make when they empower (or disempower) certain presumed local actors, institutions and practices.[72] Peacebuilding, in short, has become the locale where both 'international assistance' and 'local acquiescence, co-option or resistance' can be located. This complexity of dynamics has been termed the 'infrapolitics of peacebuilding'.[73]

72   Niagale Bagayoko, Eboe Hutchful & Robin Luckham. 2016. 'Hybrid security governance in Africa: rethinking the foundations of security, justice and legitimate public authority', Conflict, Security & Development, 16:(1), pp. 1-32; Newman, Edward (2013) The violence of statebuilding in historical perspective: implications for peacebuilding, Peacebuilding, 1 (1), pp. 141-157.

73   Richmond. 2011

Solutions to wicked problems are not true or false, but good or bad.

Page 23

HAS PEACEBUILDING BECOME A WICKED PROBLEM?

In 2020, the UN undertook a review of its peacebuilding activities,[74] taking stock of the progress made over the first 15 years of its PBA, with a special focus on field-level engagements. From 2006 to 2021, the Peacebuilding Fund (PBF) allocated nearly $1.67 billion to 65 recipient countries. Of the 20 states that received funding for its programmatic work between 2020 and 2024, 15 were in Africa.[75] However, in the African round of consultations for the review, some of the critical conclusions were that: 'Local peacebuilders are not sufficiently involved in the identification of needs, the framing of the issues or the design of the programs and results frameworks.'[76] Furthermore, those who were consulted for the report had little knowledge of the sustaining peace concept. Those who are more familiar with the concept feel that while the degree to which it emphasises local and national ownership, 'early preventive action and system-wide cooperation, collaboration and coherence though exemplary, its implementation strategies or mechanisms were weak'.[77] This assessment raises two fundamental questions. First, what are the levels of success or effectiveness of the peacebuilding programmes launched in recipient states in Africa? And second, if they have not been as successful as intended over the past two decades, to what extent does this limited success make peacebuilding a wicked problem?

The notion of wicked problems was identified as a general barrier to the effective design and implementation of policies, as much as it was conceptualised as a special class of problem. Whatever the particular concerns of the planning or policy analytical literature, the concept of wicked problems is defined on the basis of the following ten characteristics:

1. Wicked problems are difficult to define: there is no definite formulation.
2. Wicked problems have no stopping rule.
3. Solutions to wicked problems are not true or false, but good or bad.
4. There is no immediate or ultimate test for solutions.
5. Any attempt to provide a solution has effects that may not be reversible or forgettable.

---

74 The first UN peacebuilding review was in 2015,
75 These include Burkina Faso, Burundi, Central Africa Republic, Chad, DRC, Guinea, Guinea Bissau, Liberia, Madagascar, Mali, Sierra Leone, Somalia, South Sudan, Sudan and The Gambia.
76 See ACCORD-AU. 2020. 2020 Review of the United Nations Peacebuilding Architecture African Regional Consultation Report, 30 June 2020. p. 2.
77 Ibid, p.2

6. These problems have no clear solution, and perhaps not even a set of possible solutions.
7. Every wicked problem is essentially unique.
8. Every wicked problem may be a symptom of another problem.
9. There are multiple explanations for the wicked problem.
10. The planner (policy-maker) has no right to be wrong.[78]

Due to the intractability of particular types of problems, the term 'super wicked problems' has come into play:[79] This phrase describes the nature of significant policy problems facing contemporary governments and multilateral institutions and non-governmental agencies in preventing conflict and rebuilding states for sustainable peace. Like the concept of wicked problems, the defining characteristics of 'super wicked problems' include: limited time; lack of (or only limited) central authority to manage the problem to hand; and how the problem must be resolved.

If peacebuilding has become a wicked problem in the context of the majority of those states whose problems it seeks to resolve, then it is essential to determine certain things. First, what is unique about these African cases? And second, is time running out to resolve these problems in the Sahel, especially in Mali?

---

78 Peters, B Guy. 2017. What is so wicked about wicked problems? A conceptual analysis and a research program, Policy and Society, 36 (3), September, pp. 385–396.
79 Levin, K. B., Cashore, S. Bernstein, & Auld, G. (2012). Overcoming the tragedy of super wicked problems: Constraining our future selves to ameliorate global climate change. Policy Sciences, 45, pp. 121–152.

MALI'S SLIPPERY SLOPE TO COLLAPSE

A discursive construction of insecurity in Mali reveals the reality and challenge of peacebuilding interventions.[80] Until its collapse in 2012, Mali had often been viewed as a model of democracy, functional institutions and stability on the African continent. The country had also long been acclaimed for its cultural diversity, wealth and richness, due to the immense trove of architectural traditions and historic sites represented in such ancient cities as Timbuktu, Gao, Douentza and Kidal.[81] However, the narratives surrounding Mali's reputation as a beacon of democracy and a hub of world cultural heritage sites overshadowed a more disturbing set of structural, political and economic inequalities that were eventually to come to the fore. And when they did, they diminished and threatened the very survival of the state. In 2012, Mali was plunged into a state of unexpected and unprecedented political crisis, taking most observers by surprise. What shocked observers was that the upheaval occurred barely a month before scheduled presidential elections in 2012. On 22 March 2012, a group of soldiers led by Captain Amadou Haya Sanogo overthrew the constitutionally elected president, Ahmadou Toumani Touré, in a military coup d'état.[82] Justifying the coup d'etat, the main explanation by the military for its actions was the inadequate government funding for the campaign against the 'separatist' insurrection by Tuareg rebels in the north of Mali. However, the intervention by the military elicited criticism from the Economic Community of West African States (ECOWAS) and the African Union (AU). As a result of these criticisms and the threat of sanctions, a few days after the coup, a transitional government was established, led by Dioncounda Traoré, leader of the National Assembly.[83]

The coup d'état led to an accelerated process of collapse in the North, where the Tuaregs took up arms against the state and resulting in a severe security vacuum. The Tuareg rebels, together with other armed groups such as Al-Qaeda in the Islamic Maghreb (AQIM) and Ansar Dine took advantage of this instability and

---

80 I am grateful to my former colleagues, Dr. Fiifi Edu-Afful now of American University, Washington, D.C and Dr. Festus Aubyn of WANEP, Accra, Ghana for helping me complete a much larger study for the Mali – Security Sector Horizon Scanning Study, Cranfield University.

81 See "Cultural Heritage Sites of Mali" http://www.wmf.org/project/cultural-heritage-sites-mali, [accessed 3 December 2022]

82 Kwesi Aning and Festus Aubyn, 'Managing Complex Political Dilemmas in West Africa: the Role of ECOWAS in Mali' New Routes, 2013; Dona. J. Stewart, What is next for Mali? The Roots of Conflict and Challenges to Stability. Washington: Strategic Studies Institute and U.S. Army War College Press, 2013.

83 Kwesi Aning and Ilana Axelrod. 2020.'Mali, Democracy and ECOWAS's Sanctions Regime', KAIPTC Policy Brief 9 | October 2020.

security vacuum to seise several major cities, including Timbuktu, Gao and Kidal in the north. At the invitation of the Malian president –who was concerned at the rapid southward drive of the terrorists towards the capital Bamako – the French initiated a military intervention codenamed, Operation Serval,[84] which coincided with the deployment of the African-led International Support Mission to Mali (AFISMA) in January 2013.[85] Together, these international intervention forces ousted the armed groups from the main cities in the north.

During the initial phase of this primarily military operation, the political and security situation in the country improved considerably. As a result, successful presidential and parliamentary elections were held in August and December 2013, leading to the establishment of a new government and National Assembly. State control over the entire territory of Mali was gradually restored, albeit with multiple reversals and mistrust of the role and activities of French forces. Though the discourses about stability in Mali created the impression that the security situation had improved appreciably, especially in the north, there were still sporadic attacks by the Tuareg rebels and terrorist groups like AQIM against communities, international forces and statutory security institutions. The inclusive political dialogue and reconciliation efforts with the Tuaregs and other minority groups in the north progressed in fits and starts, with absolutely no certainty about the eventual outcome. From the macroeconomic standpoint, the World Bank noted that Mali's economy was resilient, in spite of the 2012 crises, thanks to an increase in the prices paid for the country's major exports – namely gold and cotton – on the international markets.[86] Yet, the economy remained weak and subject to fluctuations of the international pricing mechanisms. With the support of donors and development partners, the government resumed the structural reform programmes initiated before the 2012 crises: such as improving transparency in public finance management, the development of social safety nets and the diversification of agricultural production.[87] Furthermore, to improve the business climate, efforts were made to combat corruption, increase access to finance and improve the quality of public infrastructure (such as education, transport and irrigation), the power supply and the judicial system.

---

84   Sergei Boeke and Bart Schuurman. 2015. 'Operation Serval: the French Intervention in Mali', https://www.leidensecurityandglobalaffairs.nl/articles/operation-serval-the-french-intervention-in-mali ; Michael Shurkin. 2014. France's War in Mali - Lessons for an Expeditionary Army. https://www.rand.org/pubs/research_reports/RR770.html

85   Security Council Authorizes Deployment of African-Led International Support Mission in Mali for Initial Year-Long Period, 20 December 2012 Security Council SC/10870 at https://press.un.org/en/2012/sc10870.doc.htm

86   World Bank, "The Malian Economy Holds Steady in the Face of Crisis" http://www.worldbank.org/en/news/feature/2013/03/14/the-malian-economy-holds-steady-in-the-face-of-crisis, [accessed 3 December 2014]

87   Milan Cuc, "Mali on the Mend as Reforms Resume after Security Crisis" http://www.imf.org/external/pubs/ft/survey/so/2013/int123013a.htm, [3 December 2014].

POLITICAL CONTEXT

Until the 2012 political upheavals, Mali was hailed as a beacon of democracy in Francophone West Africa. But the political crises proved that the country's democracy was no more than an illusion. To better comprehend the reality of its political context, the historical trajectory of its democratic development is traced from the pre-colonial period to the present.

PRE-COLONIAL PERIOD

Present-day Mali has a rich history as one of the three famous and prosperous ancient West African empires: the Ghana, Mali (Malinké) and Songhai empires. The Mali Empire arose after the collapse of the ancient Ghana Empire in the twelfth century.[88] Geographically, it was located on the upper and middle Niger River. It was renowned for its gold resources, ivory, salt and slaves, and became a centre of trans-Saharan trade (especially the cities of Timbuktu and Djenné), Islamic learning and culture. The Mali Empire was founded by the Malinké ruler, Sundiata Keïta in the hirteenth century.[89] It reached its height in 1325, under the great ruler Mansa Kankan Musa I, who made a famous pilgrimage to Mecca in 1324 laden with gold and slaves, just to proclaim Mali's prosperity and power.[90] The importance of his visit is well captured by Davidson, Buah and Ajayi, who posit that:

> Musa's Pilgrimage to Mecca became famous. He began it in 1324. His magnificent journey through the Egyptian capital of Cairo was long remembered with admiration and surprise throughout Egypt and Arabia, for Musa took with him so much gold, and gave away so many golden gifts that the people of Cairo earned very big sums thanks to his visit. So generous was Musa with his gifts, indeed, that he upset the value of goods on the Cairo market. Gold became more plentiful and therefore worth less, and so prices rose.[91]

Mansa Kankan Musa I ruled until 1337 and was succeeded by Mansa Magha, and then Mansa Suleyman and Mari-Diata in the late 1380s.[92] The Mali Empire col-

---

88   Basil Davidson, F.K. Buah and J.F.A. Ajayi, The Growth of African Civilization: A History of West Africa 1000-1800, Longman Singapore Publishers, 1977.

89   Ibid., 1997.

90   See The Columbia Electronic Encyclopedia, 6th ed. Columbia University Press; see also 'Mali: History',www.infoplease.com/encyclopedia/world/mali history.html, [accessed 20 October, 2014].

91   Davidson, Buah and Ajayi, 1997, p.50

92   Albert Adu Boahen, Topics in West African History. London: Harlow, 1966; Albert Adu Boahen, Beiträgen von J., B Webster and M. Tidy, The Revolutionary Years: West Africa since 1800. London, 1980 Longman Group

lapsed at the end of 1400, following succession disputes after Mari-Diata's rule, to be supplanted by the Songhai Empire. This new empire controlled the Timbuktu–Gao region in the fifteenth century, but also collapsed in the face of both internal and external pressures, including a Moroccan Berber invasion in 1591. The fall of the Songhai Empire marked the end of the region's role as a trading centre. It broke up into petty states after the Moroccan invasion and a subsequent incursion by the Tuaregs and Fulanis. Two Muslim states – the Toucouleur Empire of al-Hajj Umar (1794–1864) and the empire of Samori Toure (1870–1898) – ruled the region, before being conquered by French colonial forces at the end of the nineteenth century.

FRENCH COLONIAL ERA

Mali (which at the time included parts of Mauritania, Senegal, Niger and Burkina Faso) became a French colony in 1904.[93] It was renamed French Sudan (Soudan français) and became part of the Federation of French West Africa, which was administered by a governor-general based in Senegal. French Sudan supplied labour to France's colonies on the coast of West Africa, and became an important source of raw materials (such as cotton and peanuts) bound for Paris. However, the French paid little attention to the territory and failed to develop the area, other than to construct a few roads and railways to transport trade goods to the sea.[94]

After the Second World War, nationalist independence movements began to gain momentum across French West Africa, due to the people's growing dissatisfaction with the exploitative nature of the colonial system. In an attempt to address the concerns of the people, certain reforms were made under the new constitution of the Fourth Republic of France. These included African representation in the French National Assembly and the increased participation of Africans in local governance councils in French West Africa.[95] Despite the reforms, resistance to French colonial rule continued. Hence, in 1956, the French passed the *loi cadre* (enabling law), which granted local government for individual territories in French West Africa.[96] In 1958, French Sudan obtained internal autonomy, and the territory became an autonomous state within the French Community, known as the Sudanese Republic. Mali joined with Senegal in 1959 to form the Mali Federation. However, this federation collapsed after Senegal seceded on 20 August 1960, due to political differences. Following this, what previously constituted the Sudanese Republic was renamed

---

93   See 'Mali: French Colonial Rule and Independence', http://berkleycenter.georgetown.edu/essays/mali-french-colonial-rule-and-independence, [accessed 12 November 2014].
94   'Mali: French Colonial Rule and Independence'; Albert Adu Boahen, J. F. Ade Ajayi, Topics in West African History, London: Longman Group, 1986.
95   Stephen Wooten, 'The French in West Africa: Early Contact to Independence' http://www.africa.upenn.edu/K-12/French_16178.html, [accessed 20 October 2014].
96   See http://africanhistory.about.com/od/mali/p/MaliHist1.htm, [accessed 25 October 2014].

Mali on 22 September 1960, and Modibo Keïta[97] of the socialist Sudanese Union-African Democratic Party (US-RDA) served as its first president.[98]

INDEPENDENCE AND BEYOND

After attaining independence from France, President Modibo Keïta instituted a one-party socialist state from 1960 to 1968. As a pan-Africanist, seeking to promote African unity, Keïta joined the president of Guinea, Sékou Touré, and the president of Ghana, Kwame Nkrumah, to form the Union of the States of Western Africa. He also played an important role in drafting the Charter of the Organisation of African Unity (OAU) and pursued a foreign policy of non-alignment, although he clandestinely supported the communist bloc in international affairs. In 1962, Keïta severed ties with the French Community, replaced French civil servants with Africans, and established close diplomatic and economic ties with the Eastern (communist) bloc countries.[99] He also withdrew from the Franc Zone and adopted a non-convertible national currency. Key sectors of the economy – such as trade and agriculture – were also nationalised. On trade especially, SOMIEX (Malian Import and Export Company) was established to manage the export of Malian products and the import of manufactured goods and their distribution across the country.

A few years after withdrawing from the French Community, the failure (or limited success) of the nationalisation policies created serious economic and financial difficulties in Mali.[100] It led to high inflation and growing dissatisfaction among the population, especially among the peasants and businessmen. Efforts by Keïta to restore economic stability resulted in devaluation of the Malian currency, a return to the Franc Zone and permission for French administrators to assume a supervisory role in the economy.[101] These policy changes, coupled with Keïta's radical socialist political and economic policies, led to widespread public discontent and general unrest, and made him unpopular within his own party. To suppress his opponents and the growing public resentment of his government, President Keïta formed the *milice populaire* (the US-RDA militia). However, the arrest and imprisonment of several dissenting politicians and army officers by the militia resulted in a bloodless military coup on 19 November 1968, led by Lieutenant Moussa Traoré. Keïta spent the rest of his life in military detention, until his death on 17 May 1977.

---

97   Keïta was the first African vice president of the national assembly in Paris and also served in two French cabinets.

98   Encyclopædia Britannica 'Modibo Keita' http://www.britannica.com/EBchecked/topic/314244/Modibo-Keita, [accessed 11 November 2014].

99   See 'Mali: History', http://www.infoplease.com/encyclopedia/world/mali-history.html#ixzz-3JeKnz6FV, [accessed on 20 October, 2014].

100   BBC, 'Mali Profile' http://www.bbc.com/news/world-africa-13881372, [accessed on 27 October, 2014].

101   http://www.infoplease.com/country/mali.html#ixzz3JVwsfyoz, [accessed on 10 October, 2014]

After the overthrow of Keïta, a fourteen-member Military Committee of National Liberation, led by Lieutenant Moussa Traoré as head of state and Captain Yoro Diakité as prime minister, was formed to rule the country. However, disagreements led to the removal of two officers – including Captain Yoro Diakité – in 1971, and four others accused of planning a coup in 1978.[102] Under the presidency of Traoré, the socialist policies of the previous regime were discontinued and political activities were banned. The country also faced a prolonged drought in the early 1970s, which hindered agriculture/crop production and killed thousands of head of livestock. The drought – which was more pronounced in the Sahel region – resulted in famine, disease, poverty, thousands of deaths and the forced migration of many people southward. In 1974, there was also a border dispute over the ownership of the Agacher Strip (a border region of about 1,150 square miles or 3,000 square km) between Mali and Upper Volta, now Burkina Faso. The matter was subsequently resolved following mediation efforts by the OAU. However, the agreement was not sustainable, and the dispute re-emerged in 1985. This time, the matter was referred to the International Court of Justice, which divided the territory in 1986 to the satisfaction of both parties.[103]

To return the country to civilian rule, a new constitution was adopted in 1974 following a referendum, and this paved the way for a national election to be held in 1979. The election was won by Lieutenant Moussa Traoré, who led the military-sponsored political party, the Malian People's Democratic Union (UDPM). He was re-elected in 1985, and UDPM (the sole legal party) took all 82 seats in the National Assembly.[104] President Traoré consolidated his hold on power by repressing all coup attempts, banning all political parties and dealing drastically with protests. He maintained close diplomatic and economic relations with both France and the communist bloc and improved the country's relationship with the West, especially the United States of America.[105] Having been in power for 23 years, Moussa Traoré was overthrown in 1991 in yet another coup d'*état* led by Amadou Toumani Touré, putting an end to over two decades of Traoré's dictatorship in Mali. Traoré's overthrow followed months of mass uprisings and street demonstrations led by labour unions, students and unemployed university graduates in major urban centres over his repressive regime and the deteriorating economy.[106] According to Soumana Sacko, a former Malian finance minister and also prime minister:

---

102   Alistair Boddy-Evans, 'Malian Politician and Military Strongman' http://africanhistory.about.com/od/mali/a/Bio-Moussa-Traore.htm, [accessed 15 November 2014].
103   Kathleen M. Baker, 2014, 'Republic of Mali' http://www.britannica.com/EBchecked/topic/360071/Mali/279097/The-arts#toc279101, [accessed 15 October 2014].
104   Alistair Boddy-Evans, 'Malian Politician and Military Strongman' http://africanhistory.about.com/od/mali/a/Bio-Moussa-Traore.htm, [accessed 14 November 2022].
105   Alistair Boddy-Evans, 'Malian Politician and Military Strongman'
106   Soumana Sacko, 'Crisis in Mali: Lessons from an ongoing democratic transition' the Legatum Institute (LI) transitional forum, case study, February 2014.

> The demonstrators had been inspired by the Traoré regime's unwillingness to open up the political space and accept multiparty democracy; its inability to address pressing socio-economic demands stemming from mass poverty and growing unemployment among secondary school and university graduates; its inability to clear the arrears in civil service pay and meet pay demands from the labour unions; and its failure to stamp out corruption.[107]

These demonstrations and increasing public discontent started the process towards the transition to multi-party democracy.

TRANSITION TO MULTI-PARTY DEMOCRACY

A transitional military committee headed by Amadou Toumani Touré was set up after the overthrow of Traoré to lay the institutional foundations for a return to civilian rule. It is instructive to note that Mali's transition to multi-party democracy was connected and inspired by the general wave of democratisation in Africa after the end of the Cold War. Thus, in the early 1990s, the continent was characterised by a general trend towards pluralistic politics and multi-party electoral competition.[108] Therefore, most military dictators or autocratic leaders on the continent were forced either to relinquish power to a democratically elected president or to revise their constitutions to allow multi-party democracy. Mali was no exception to this; hence, when the military seised power in 1991, it had no choice but to return the country to civilian rule due to international pressure.

In order to draw up a new constitution for the Third Republic, the transitional government organised a National Conference from 29 July to 12 August 1991. This gave the people a unique opportunity to construct a shared vision for a new democratic future for Mali. Following a series of deliberations and debates, a new constitution was drafted. Key provisions in it guaranteed human rights and civil liberties, provided for a multi-party semi-presidential system, with separation of powers, as well as checks and balances; a charter of political parties; and a new electoral code, which made room for independent candidates with no party affiliation to run for election.[109] The draft constitution was overwhelmingly approved by referendum on 12 January 1992.

---

107   Soumana Sako op. cit.
108   Mathias, Hounkpe and Alioune, B. Gueye., 'The Role of Security Forces in the Electoral Process: The Case of Six West African Countries' (Lagos: Friedrich- Ebert-Stiftung, 2010); Said, Adejumobi, 'Elections in Africa: A fading Shadow of Democracy?' International Political Science Review, 2000, 21(1),
109   Soumana Sako, op. cit.

On the basis of this new constitution, local, parliamentary and presidential elections were held in February, March and April 1992, respectively, with Alpha Oumar Konaré of the Alliance for Democracy being chosen as Mali's first democratically elected president: he received 69.01 per cent of the vote, beating the US-RDA candidate, Tiéoulé Mamadou Konaté. His election marked the beginning of the Third Republic and raised the hopes of Malians for a more democratic future. President Konaré made several attempts to rebuild Mali's democratic institutions and revamp the economy. The government also invested in infrastructure development in areas such as roads, bridges, schools and low-cost housing.

However, these efforts were hampered by a weak economy, inflation, drought, desertification, a bloated civil service, unemployment, decreased foreign aid and the French government's devaluation of the CFA franc in 1994.[110] These challenges resulted in economic hardships and several student riots, which often turned violent. From 1990 to 1992, the government also faced a continuing Tuareg rebellion in the northern part of the country. This crisis was caused by Tuareg rebels who returned from Libya and Algeria, where they had migrated during droughts in the 1970s and 1980s.[111] The Tuaregs rebelled against alleged government usurpation of their land and suppression of their culture and language.[112] Following political negotiations between the government and the Tuaregs, a National Pact was signed on 11 April 1992, bringing a political settlement. According to Sacko, the National Pact provided for a decentralised system of government and gave 'special status' to the northern regions, by allowing for local management of regional affairs.[113] Former Tuareg rebels were also integrated into the armed forces and civilian sectors of public administration, and fiscal incentives were provided to attract investment to the northern regions and address socio-economic development problems.[114]

However, this could not permanently address the problems of the Tuaregs, due to the limited success in implementation of the National Pact. In other words, the fragile peace with the Tuaregs did not last very long, as the crisis resumed in 2006. In May 1997, President Konaré was re-elected virtually unopposed, amid charges of electoral fraud and human rights abuses.[115] The opposition parties boycotted the elections, on account of a lack of reliable and comprehensive voter registration lists. They vowed not to recognise Mr Konaré as the legitimate president of Mali and

---

110   Kathleen M. Baker, op. cit.
111   Kalifa Keita, 'Conflict and Conflict Resolution in the Sahel: The Tuareg Insurgency in Mali,' Small Wars & Insurgencies 9, no. 3 (1998); Devon DB, 'the Crisis in Mali: A Historical Perspective on the Tuareg People', Global Research, 1 February, 2013, http://www.globalresearch.ca/the-crisis-in-mali-a-historical-perspective-on-the-tuareg-people/5321407, [accessed 17 November 2014].
112   Kalifa Keita, op. cit.,
113   Soumana Sako, op. cit.,
114   Kalifa Keita, op. cit p. 8
115   Kathleen M. Baker, op. cit.,

launched a civil disobedience campaign that lasted over a year.[116] Overall, Konaré's tenure as president is noted for the restoration of democracy, his management of the Tuareg rebellion and his decentralisation of government.

Presidential elections in April and May 2002 resulted in the victory of Amadou Touré, the former interim military ruler, who contested the election as an independent candidate. He won 64 per cent of the total vote. His victory came as a result of the overwhelming support he enjoyed from the majority of political parties and civil society groups, who at the time wanted a leader who could tackle the country's mounting socio-economic hardships and reunite the Malian people. Amadou Touré was re-elected for a second term in 2007, but this time around he won with a huge 71 per cent of the vote.[117] Like his predecessors, his administration also faced economic problems and various conflicts, including renewed Tuareg rebellion in 2006 and disputes between Guinean and Malian villagers over land rights, which in 2007 resulted in injury, death and loss of property.[118] Poverty also worsened between 2006 and 2010 in Bamako, leading to rapid rural-to-urban migration.[119] Widespread corruption in public offices similarly eroded the legitimacy of state democratic institutions, and it was at this time that radical Islamism started to take root in Malian society.

THE 2012 POLITICAL CRISIS AND ITS AFTERMATH

Emboldened by the presence of well-equipped combatants returning from Libya in the wake of the fall of Muammar Gaddafi's regime in 2011, the National Movement for the Liberation of Azawad (MNLA), a Tuareg rebel group, initiated a series of attacks on government forces in northern Mali. They carried these out with other Islamic armed groups, including Ansar Dine, Movement for Oneness and Jihad in West Africa (MUJAO) and AQIM.[120] The rebels and armed groups scored a number of surprising victories, taking over a number of towns and chasing the Malian soldiers out of some of their garrisons in the north.[121] The relative guerrilla success of the armed groups deeply angered and demoralised the ill-equipped Malian soldiers, who accused the government of inadequate material and logistical support to fight the rebels.

Subsequently, a mutiny at the Kati military camp on 21 March 2012, near the presidential palace in the capital city Bamako. Carried out by disaffected soldiers

116   Soumana Sako op. cit.,
117   See 'Profile: Amadou Toumani Toure' http://www.aljazeera.com/news/
         africa/2012/03/20123229824215677.html, [accessed 20 November 2014].
118   Soumana Sako op. cit.,
119   Ibid.,
120   Kwesi Aning and Festus Aubyn, 'Managing Complex Political Dilemmas in West Africa: the Role
         of ECOWAS in Mali' New Routes, 2013
121   Adam Nossiter,'Soldiers Overthrow Mali Government in Setback for Democracy in Africa' http://
         www.nytimes.com/2012/03/23/world/africa/mali-coup-france-calls-for-elections.html?page-
         wanted=all&_r=0, [accessed 15 November 2014].

from the units defeated by the armed groups in the north, this resulted in the over-throw of President Ahmadou Toumani Touré in the military coup d'état led by Captain Amadou Haya Sanogo. After seising power, the military junta, also known as the National Committee for the Restoration of Democracy and State, suspended the constitution, arrested ministers, closed Mali's land and air borders and implemented a curfew. The coup d'état occurred at a time when the country was preparing for a presidential election in April 2012. Although what sparked the coup was the rising tide of discontent over government failure to equip the military to deal effectively with a 'separatist' insurrection by Tuareg rebels, poor governance and grievances over deteriorating socio-economic conditions in the country also contributed. Thus, prior to the coup, there were public protests over the poor political and military management of the Tuareg rebellion, issues of widespread corruption in government, nepotism, mismanagement of natural resources, deteriorating socio-economic conditions and proliferation of arms from the Sahel region.[122] However, the government failed to take proactive measures to respond adequately to these challenges.[123] The military junta just tapped into these long-simmering problems. A few days after the coup, the swift intervention of ECOWAS and the AU forced the military to relinquish power,[124] leading to the formation of a transitional government led by interim President Dioncounda Traoré, that was tasked, among other things, with returning the country to constitutional rule.

Meanwhile, the coup accelerated the collapse of the state in the north. A few days after the coup, the MNLA, together with other armed groups such as Ansar Dine, MUJAO and AQIM, took advantage of the power vacuum to declare an independent 'Islamic State of Azawad' on 6 April 2012.[125] For the 18 months that these armed groups controlled northern Mali, they imposed a strict interpretation of sharia law on the population, perpetrated grave human rights abuses (including child recruitment, summary executions and sexual violence), mounted attacks on schools and hospitals and engaged in the destruction of religious, historical and cultural sites.[126]

---

122 Ibid.
123 See WANEP, 'MALI: Managing the Damage of a Complex' http://www.wanep.org, [accessed 3 October 2012]
124 ECOWAS invoked its principle of Zero Tolerance for power obtained by unconstitutional means, as enshrined in the Supplementary Protocol on Democracy and Good Governance and imposed political, diplomatic, economic and financial sanctions on members of the military junta to force immediate restoration of constitutional order. It was these targeted sanctions that forced the military to relinquish power for a transitional government to be put in place.
125 See Aning and Aubyn op.cit p.10, 'Security Situation in West Africa' Europaworld.com, General Survey, 2012; see UNSC, 2014, Report of the Secretary-General on Children and Armed Conflict in Mali, /2014/267/, 14 April 2014. New York: United Nations
126 Human Rights Watch, 'Mali: Islamist Armed Groups Spread Fear in North', http://www. hrw.org, [accessed 12 August 2014]; UNSC, 2014, Report of the Secretary-General on Children and Armed Conflict in Mali, /2014/267/, 14 April 2014. New York: United Nations.

To deal with the Tuareg separatist rebellion and the armed groups in the north, the UN used UNSC Resolution 2085 (2012) to authorise the deployment of the African-led AFISMA, in order to (among other things) support the Malian authorities in recovering control of the areas in the north from the armed groups. Under Resolution 2085, AFISMA was supposed to be deployed in September 2013. However, following an unexpected advance by the rebel and terrorist groups southwards, towards Bamako, in January 2013, the Malian transitional authorities requested intervention by France to neutralise the threat.[127] In January 2013, soon after the French intervention, ECOWAS and the AU deployed the AFISMA forces in support of the French military and the Malian Defence Forces to recover the rebel-held regions in the north.[128] By the end of January 2013, state control had been restored in most of the major northern towns, such as Diabaly, Douentza, Gao, Konna and Timbuktu. While some of the armed groups fled north, into the Adrar des Ifoghas Mountains, others blended into the local communities, since when they have employed tactics of asymmetric warfare to destabilise the region.[129]

Following the recapture of northern Mali from the rebels, presidential elections were held on 28 July 2013. The people of Mali had 28 candidates to choose from during this election, but the front-runners were Ibrahim Boubacar Keïta and Soumaïla Cissé, who won 39.23 per cent and 19.44 per cent, respectively, of the vote in the first round of elections.[130] In the second round, held on 11 August 2013, Ibrahim Boubacar Keïta of the Rally for Mali (Rassemblement pour le Mali – RPM) won decisively, with 77.7 per cent (2,354,693) of the vote, against Soumaïla Cissé's (Union for the Republic and Democracy – URD) 23.6 per cent (679,258). Accordingly, he became president of Mali.[131] The legislative elections on 24 November 2013 and 15 December 2013 also gave the RPM and its allies control of 78 per cent of the seats in the National Assembly.[132] Imperfect as they were, the presidential and legislative elections put an end to months of uncertainty and more than a year of political turmoil in the country.

---

127   See Mehari T. Maru, 2013, 'AFISMA: Military ahead of Politics http://studies.aljazeera.net/en/repo rts/2013/02/20132148940690455, [accessed 3 October 2022]
128   Festus Aubyn, 2014, 'Policing And Peace Operations In Africa: Reflections On MINUSMA' unpublished paper
129   For more information see UNSC, 2014, Report of the Secretary-General on Children and Armed Conflict in Mali, /2014/267/, 14 April 2014. New York: United Nations.
130   Morten Boas, 2013, 'Mali 2013: A Year of Elections and Further Challenges' http://www.e-ir. info/2013/12/22/mali-2013-a-year-of-elections-and-further-challenges/, [accessed 12 November 2014]; Ba, Boubacar and Morten Bøås (2013) The Mali Presidential Elections: Outcomes and Challenges, Oslo: Noref (Noref Report October 2013).
131   Adam Nossiter and Peter Tinti, 2013, 'Mali Holds Elections After Year of Turmoil' http://www.nytimes.com/2013/07/29/world/africa/mali-holds-elections-after-year-of-turmoil.html, [accessed 10 November 2014].
132   The National Democratic Institute, 2013, 'Mali' https://www.ndi.org/mali, [accessed 12 November 2014].

INTERNATIONAL PEACEBUILDING ENGAGEMENTS

Mali's history, politics, geography and eventual collapse in 2012 contain vignettes of how the production of knowledge about particular states, conflicts and the potential threats they pose to the wider international community subsequently inform how peacebuilding interventions are designed and implemented. Such a discursive construction of threats, Newman argues, contributes to an 'inter-subjectively shared construction of weak and conflict prone states as a threat, and peacebuilding as the response'.[133] A subjective construction and use of peacebuilding (with its multiple array of options) becomes a response framework that elevates the constructed insecurity above the realm of ordinary politics; that represents 'a form of securitization … loosely applied and … only partially successful'.[134] Furthermore, the argument that '[t]he securitization of peacebuilding has brought obvious benefits' that result in increased funding and humanitarian assistance helps propel forgotten crises to the fore. The net impact of such obvious benefits, it is argued, especially when insecurity are discursively constructed, is that 'viewing conflict, poor governance and underdevelopment in the developing world as a threat to Western interests has brought much needed resources, aid and capacity building to some of these countries'. Due to its crises since 2012, Mali is certainly an obvious candidate for examining how peacebuilding as (re)building critical state institutions is undertaken. This involves reforming the statutory security institutions through security sector reform (SSR). Such processes in a conflicted-affected state is viewed by powerful states as a strategic international action.[135] For this discussion, endeavours to stabilise Mali through reform of its armed forces will be used as an empirical study.

---

133 Newman, 2010, op cit., p.314. See the earlier mention of Susan Woodward's concerns about the framing of the debate as to what is weak, fragile and collapsed and how defines the nature of response that invariably worsens the situation or poses a danger to states so defined.

134 Ibid, p. 314

135 Ibid, p. 313; See Aning, K and E. Lartey. 2014. 'The role of RECs in peacebuilding in Africa: past experiences and the way forward' Cairo Policy Briefs, No. 3, November at https://www.cccpa-eg.org/publications-details/353 . In Mali alone, UN has deployed a stabilisation mission in Mali (MINUSMA); France a regional counterterrorism force, Operation Barkhane, (apart from earlier forces) and since early 2020, a European Task Force Takuba deployed under French command; the European Union (EU) runs one military training mission in Mali, and two civilian missions in Mali and Niger, all focused on security force and rule of law assistance; and the United States and various other Western countries provide bilateral forms of security force assistance to the region's states. Furthermore, since 2017, the G5 Sahel states (Burkina Faso, Chad, Mali, Mauritania, and Niger) have deployed a 5,200-strong counterterrorism Joint Force which operates along the region's porous borders. See, Wilén, Nina and Paul D. Williams. 2022. 'What Are the International Military Options for the Sahel?', at https://theglobalobservatory.org/2022/04/what-are-the-international-military-options-for-the-sahel/ . There is also the Multinational Joint Taskforce (MNJTF)

A little background to the international endeavours to rebuild and reconstruct the Malian state through SSR is in order. Through its regionalisation, the conflict in Mali has inevitably drawn neighbouring and proximate states into an ever-widening and transforming zone of insecurity. Worsening domestic and international tensions and transnational organised crimes have spread across Mali, Burkina Faso and Niger, (especially in the Liptako-Gourma area, which has increasingly become the epicentre of the Sahel crisis).[136] Furthermore, with its insecurity expanding to gradually engulf Burkina Faso and spreading towards the coastal states, Mali has become the epicentre of regional insecurity, accounting for nearly 60 per cent of all violent jihadist incidents in the Sahel in 2021, with significant influx of refugees fleeing the armed conflicts.

With worsening armed insurgency and multiple coups d'état since 2012, Mali's fragile democratic and security developments have been gravely undermined. Obvious warning signs were neglected, such as deteriorating socio-economic conditions, worsening and widening insecurity and corruption. The country itself, ECOWAS[137] and its international partners are all now facing critical challenges in stabilising the state. Earlier on, I argued that the nature of Mali's challenges meant that 'no stakeholder in the country should be left outside these process' of reconciliation and reconstruction, and that there was a 'historic duty to ensure peace',[138] based on Mali's location in the Sahel – a duty that has experienced multiple fits and starts. Mali, once described as an example of West Africa's most stable transitional democracies, collapsed in spectacular fashion in 2012, raising critical questions about the types of analytical variables that are used to produce knowledge about democratic stability and to assess appropriate response options in African conflicts and during periods of instability.

Today, Mali epitomises a regional insecurity hotspot. Questions about what went wrong and why – and particularly how specific knowledge about the Malian situation was produced that then informed the subsequent decision by ECOWAS, the AU, EU, France and eventually the UN and a host of other bilateral and multilateral forces within a congested security space with multiple actors seeking to build peace in Mali – substantiates the earlier arguments about the need to understand

---

136 Aning, K and L. Amedzrator. 2014.'Security in the Sahel: Linking the Atlantic to the Mediterranean', in Riccardo Alcaro and Nicoletta Pirozzi, (Eds) Transatlantic Security from the Sahel to the Horn of Africa., (Rome: IAI Research Papers No. 12); 2014.'The Economics of Militancy and Islamist Extremism in the Sahel' in Political stability and security in West and North Africa (Toronto: World Watch: Expert Notes series publication No. 2014-04-01) at www.csis-scrs.gc.ca

137 UN/ECOWAS MoU on Peacebuilding.

138 Aning, K and Festus Aubyn. 2013. ''Challenges in Mali: historic duty to ensure peace', New Routes, No. 2, (PDF) Challenges in Mali Historic duty to ensure peace, p. 24.

Africa on its own terms.[139] To get to grips with Mali's ever-evolving conflict, this paper argues for an analysis of the conflict parties' interests and alliances, as a fulcrum around which peacebuilding efforts should be undertaken. Into this complex mix of local-actor interests were superimposed external actors, who all sought to re-establish the authority of the Malian state. It is critical to look (albeit briefly) at the diverse narratives, approaches and conceptions that determined the intervention logic of the different actors.

First, France: it initially intervened in Mali under a bilateral agreement or 'invitation' from the Malian state-initiated Operation Serval in 2012, ostensibly to halt the southward progress of terrorists towards Bamako, Mali's capital. Subsequently, it became part of Operation Barkhane, a counterterrorism operation against Islamic jihadists who sought to impose their control across the Sahel region. Is halting the rapid movement of the terrorists and establishing a stable, peaceful Mali the driving interest for France? This paper argues that all the altruistic arguments about Mali concealed a more calculated approach: namely, that France's strategic interest in Mali and its neighbours is primarily economic and security related. It sought to protect its uranium mines in Niger (responsible for about 20 per cent of the fuel for France's nuclear reactors). Though the narrative surrounding France's 'humanitarian' intervention in Mali was it sought to prevent Mali's failure as a state (due to the Islamist groups mentioned earlier), its interests in Mali and Niger (to where it has relocated its forces, after pulling them out of Mali) – and indeed Africa as a whole – drive its actions.[140]

Second, the European Union Training Mission in Mali (EUTM) was established in 2013, with the aim of 'train[ing] the Malian armed forces ... under the framework of the EU Common Security and Defence Policy (CSDP)'. Now on its fifth ro-

---

139   The ECOWAS Conflict Prevention Framework (ECPF), which is its main vehicle for its peacebuilding strategy. It is a 'comprehensive operational conflict prevention and peacebuilding strategy that enables the ECOWAS system and member states to draw upon human and financial resources at the regional (including civil society and the private sector)', ECOWAS, 2006. The ECOWAS Conflict Prevention Framework, Article 7, In general, two broad categories of roles can be associated with the RECs, and in this particular case ECOWAS: these are the direct and indirect roles, which respectively correspond, first, to norm setting, and secondly, to norm execution role in peacebuilding. Aning and Lartey, ibid. p. 4. The components are: early-warning; preventive diplomacy; democracy and political governance; human rights and the rule of law; media; natural resource governance; cross-border initiatives; security governance; practical disarmament; women, peace, and security; youth empowerment; the ECOWAS Standby Force (ESF); humanitarian assistance; and peace education (the Culture of Peace).

140   Powell, Nathaniel. 2022. 'Why France failed in Mali', https://warontherocks.com/2022/02/why-france-failed-in-mali/ February 21, accessed 17.11.22; 'Martina Schwikowski. 2022. 'Europe's troop withdrawal leaves Mali in limbo', https://www.dw.com/en/europes-troop-withdrawal-leaves-mali-in-limbo/a-60817940 17 February; Jason Burke. 2022. 'International troops quit Mali as violence and Moscow's influence grow', https://www.theguardian.com/world/2022/nov/17/troops-quit-mali-violence-moscow-influence 17 November

tation, this mission, which was approved on 23 March 2020, was supposed to last for four years (until 18 May 2024). Its objective was to:

> deliver advice to the Ministry of Defence (MoD) and the Malian Armed Forces (MaAF) authorities and staff, and military education and training to the MaAF. [The end result of such training, was for the] Malian authorities to reach a self-sustainable MaAF able to contribute to the defence of the Malian territory and to ensure the protection of the Malian population. [Furthermore, it] will deliver advice, education and training to the G5S Joint Force to support its operationalization and support the national armed forces of the G5 Sahel countries.[141]

Third, yet another multilateral creation in the Sahel is the G5 Sahel force, deployed in Mali to monitor developments. Furthermore, both the AU and the UN are significant players in the country. The UN, for example, has its United Nations Multidimensional Integrated Stabilization Mission in Mali (MINUSMA), established by UNSC Resolution 2100 of 25 April 2013 to support political processes in that country and carry out a number of security-related tasks. Furthermore, it supervises implementation of the 2015 Agreement for Peace and Reconciliation in Mali, known as the Algiers Process.

What drives the multiple actors in Mali, and what are their domestic imperatives and calculations, couched as a humanitarian rationale for intervention? Why have all these supposedly well-intentioned efforts to bring peace and stability to Mali failed to deliver their critical objectives, and after a decade of tweaks, resulted in a situation that the UN itself characterises as 'a poisonous climate marked by suspicion and mistrust, with a continuous narrowing of civic space, the hardening of the Malian transitional authorities, and a malaise that does not spare international partners'?[142] An overview of the competing and clashing national agendas explains that:

> Different external actors have varied motives for deploying forces across the Sahel. They include reducing refugee flows into Europe, degrading jihadist groups, improving local security forces, promoting multilateralism through the UN, reinforcing

---

141 EU TRAINING Mission Mali (EUTM Mali) at https://eutmmali.eu/wp-content/uploads/2022/01/20220113_Fact-Sheet-EUTM-sans-elections-22FEB_ENG.pdf.
142 'Mali: Security situation deteriorates, human rights concerns rise', at https://news.un.org/en/story/2022/08/1124692 accessed on 2 November 2022.

> the EU's security identity, and strengthening partnerships with
> allies such as France and the United States. Yet, while refugee
> flows have decreased, jihadist groups have multiplied, casual-
> ties from organized violence have significantly increased, and
> Russian mercenaries have moved into the region, invited in by
> Mali's junta. These developments raise difficult questions about
> whether and in what configuration external forces should remain
> in the region. The region's crises have also drifted further from
> the public spotlight with considerable media attention prioritizing
> the war in Ukraine.[143]

Mali's descent into further instability from 2020 onwards (there have been two coups since 2020) shows the need for critical assessment of how peacebuilding interventions are undertaken. First, is the need to engage with the dominant understandings of building peace through a narrow grasp of who the critical actors, second, who the constituent parts of the Malian state are, and third, who should be included in the peacebuilding process.

The cocktail of bilateral and multilateral packages provided to Mali sought to: 'educate', 'train', 'protect', 'self-sustain' and 'support' were conceptualised within the context of the prevailing understanding of the state and its constituent parts. For a state that has, since 2012, been perceived as 'failing', 'failed' or with 'ungoverned spaces' cannot be the sole mediating partner in rebuilding and reconstructing peace. As argued by Abrahamsen, when a state fails, it is no longer just a dysfunctional state in which only the local citizens are affected. Instead, it becomes a 'free trade zone for the underworld' and needs to be effectively regulated[144]. Herein lies the fallacy (and weakness) of locating peacebuilding interventions within a purely statist interpretation that does not always represent the reality in African states. Until peacebuilding knowledge is decolonised, it is unlikely that the reproduction of the conditions that foster crises in the first instance will be averted. These are the conversations that Olonisakin and colleagues argue for[145].

More than a decade after Mali's collapse in 2012 and the first in a series of bilateral and multilateral interventions, the country's security situation is still dire.[146]

---

143   Wilen and Williams, op cit.
144   Rita Abrahamsen. 2005. 'Blair's Africa: The Politics of Securitization and Fear', Alternatives, 30,
        pp. 55ff.
145   Olonisakin, et. al. op cit.
146   Ena Dion and Joseph Sany. 2021. 'After Two Coups, Mali Needs Regional Support to Bolster
        Democracy Regional and international actors will need to prioritize locally devised and accepted
        solutions to tackle the roots causes of Mali's troubles', at https://www.usip.org/publica-
        tions/2021/12/after-two-coups-mali-needs-regional-support-bolster-democracy, 9 December.

Its security in the central part of the country continues to be precarious; insecurity there and in the tri-border area between Mali, Burkina Faso and Niger continues to undermine the restoration of state authority. Islamic State in the Greater Sahara (ISGS) and its affiliate groups exploit the security voids and fight for territorial control.[147] In a recent report by the UN Secretary-General to the Security Council, there is a recognition of the urgent 'need to restore State authority and rebuild trust with local communities'.[148] How can this best be done?

---

147   See, Pieter van Ostaeyen and Kwesi Aning, 2023. 'Status of ISWAP and ISGS in West Africa and Sahel', at CEP-KAS_Paper 2_Status of ISWAP and ISGS in West Africa and Sahel,_June 2023. pdf (counterextremism.com).

148   UNSC. 2022. Report of the Secretary-General on the situation in Mali (S/2022/731), 3 October.

Reflexivity is about the self-awareness of one's positionality as knowledge producer and the unequal power dynamics between oneself and the research subjects.

Page 43

Geneva, July 2023. Delegates from Mali and other countries at the Opening of the World Intellectual Property Organization (WIPO) Assemblies. Photo: WIPO..

POSITIONALITY AND REFLEXIVITY IN PEACEBUILDING?

In the introduction, I questioned how knowledge is generated, as well as the extent to which positionality and reflexivity can contribute to defining how peace is built or formed.[149] I follow Ba's arguments in terms of the three interpretations of reflexivity in the literature: (a) positionality; (b) critique; and finally (c) practice approach. Ba argues that, 'From a positionality perspective, the object of reflection is the scholarship itself and the relationship between the scholar and the community which is the object of knowledge'[150]. Reflexivity, therefore, is about the self-awareness of one's positionality as knowledge producer and the unequal power dynamics between oneself and the research subjects. Reflexive self-awareness then consists of acknowledging the violence of writing and pursuing ways of 'conveying something that we would not otherwise have been able to hear'.[151]

In an article, Boege, Brown and Clements posit that many states outside the OECD countries are political entities that do not closely resemble the Western-style Weberian state.[152] This applies to many West African states, which in all practical forms exist as hybrid political orders where governance is carried out by the state, together with various non-state entities. To negotiate and appreciate the dynamic relationships within these entities, one needs to move beyond the Weberian notions of the state as the sole actor within a given African space and IR theorising to 'inquire into the silences of disciplines'.[153] Although the modern African state operates according to formal rules that appeal to the model of the rational-legal political order, they coexist with other forms of socio-political orders that have their roots in non-state indigenous social structures (traditional political orders).[154] The state is

---

149 Reflexivity examines one's beliefs, judgments and practices during the research process and how these may influence the research outcomes. On the other hand, positionality deals with what we know and believe in. In that sense, reflexivity is about what we do with this knowledge. See, Finlay, L. (1998) 'Reflexivity: an essential component for all research?', British Journal of Occupational Therapy, 61, (10): 453-456; Johnson, P. and Duberley, J. (2003) 'Reflexivity in management research', Journal of Management Studies, 40: 1279-1303.
150 Ba, Oumar. 2022. 'The Europeans and Americans Don't Know Africa': Of Translation, Interpretation, and Extraction', Millennium- Journal of International Studies, 50 (2), January, p.550.
151 Ba, op cit., p.553.
152 Volker Boege, Anne M. Brown, and Kevin P. Clements. (2009). 'Hybrid Political Orders, Not Fragile States'. Peace Review, 21(1), pp.13 -21.
153 Enloe, Cynthia, 1996. 'Margins, Silences and Bottom Rungs: How to Overcome the Underestimation of Power in the Study of International Relations', in Ken Booth, Steve Smith & Marysia Zalewski, Eds., International Theory: Positivism and Beyond. (Cambridge: Cambridge University Press), pp.186–202.
154 Wulf, (2007). op. cit.

only one actor among many, and 'state order' is only one of a number of orders that claim to provide public goods and services to the population.[155] The functional utility of the discussions around the hybrid notion of the state and its constituent parts goes beyond just Mali, the Sahel and West Africa: it has practical applicability in zones where the intersectionality among local, national and international encounter each other. In many places, non-state systems (such as traditional institutional structures) also function as a 'second state', delivering public goods and services in a constantly negotiated relationship with the formal institutions of governance in order to fill critical gaps in state capacity. However, there are also parallel and pre-existing jurisdictions that function and have legitimacy, despite the operations of central institutional order. This is more conspicuous with regard to the provision of peace, security and the justice function in most West African states – a development that has been characterised as having a 'simultaneity' in terms of the interactions between the modern state apparatus and the myriad non-state institutions that also provide different services. Boege and Hunt have argued that, 'important sources of everyday security – variously labelled as customary, informal, traditional or autochthonous – are commonly associated with rural spaces and attributed to the lack of presence or traction of state institutions'. However, they continue, 'these practices are not limited to peripheries; they can travel. Their structures, authority and legitimacy can be re-produced in new settings, often in response to the perturbations caused by conflict, while also changing in the course of travel'.[156] In most rural and remote peripheral areas of West Africa, where state institutions are virtually non-existent, traditional societal structures (extended families, clans, tribes, religious brotherhoods, village communities) and traditional authorities (such as village elders, headmen, clan chiefs, women leaders, religious leaders) play an important role in the everyday life of the people. These traditional structures and authorities often determine the everyday social reality of the majority of the population, due to the absence of the state and its institutions in those areas.[157] In fact, there are areas where no courts, police or other law enforcement agencies, government ministries and public services exist. In areas where they do exist, the police, for instance, are either seen as lacking capacity in terms of logistics and personnel, or even as corrupt and inefficient. The same can be said of the courts, which are also

---

155   Volker Boege, Anne Brown, Kevin Clements and Anna Nolan, On Hybrid Political Orders and Emerging States: State Formation in the Context of 'Fragility, http://www.berghof-foundation.org/fileadmin/redaktion/Publications/Handbook/Articles/boege_etal_handbook.pdf, accessed on 12 November 2022.

156   Boege, Volker and Charles T Hunt. 2020. 'On 'travelling traditions': Emplaced security in Liberia and Vanuatu', *Cooperation and Conflict*, Vol. 55, Issue 4, December, pp. 498, (italics mine).

157   Aning, Kwesi. M. Anne Brown, Volker Boege & Charles T. Hunt. 2018. *Exploring Peace formations: justice and security in post-conflict states* (London: Routledge). See particularly the introductory and concluding chapters.

often seen as inaccessible, slow to pronounce judgement, and too expensive for ordinary people to patronise.[158] Citizens are alienated from the state, and the social contract between the state and citizens has also been eroded. In many areas like Mali, the Sahel region and several parts of West Africa, the state has basically failed in its responsibility to deliver the basic law, order and security that will ensure the loyalty and participation of citizens. Hence, the people define themselves as members of a particular subnational group (kinship group, ethnicity, village), rather than perceiving themselves as citizens of a particular state.[159]

In the absence of services and the weakness of state institutions, the people have turned to their own communities for security, justice and order that they can identify with. The traditional authorities led by the chiefs and community elders have sometimes filled the security vacuum created by the absence of the state, by maintaining peace, security and justice based on local culture and customary laws. They maintain peace, law and order by applying customary laws (rather than state laws) to a number of issues that have the potential to impact on the security and development of their localities. The issues handled are multifaceted, but are usually marital problems, divorce cases, adultery or infidelity, intra- and inter-ethnic conflict, as well as inter-personal conflict.

It is, however, instructive to note that in many other places in Africa, the state operates alongside the non-state traditional authorities, and in most cases actively seeks the cooperation of traditional authority structures in enhancing the performance of state institutions. State institutions (such as the police and the judiciary) work together with the traditional authorities in several ways to provide peace, security and justice in the communities. While this relationship exists and is characterised by both cooperation and conflict, additional efforts are required to improve and deepen the relationship. Put differently, hybrid domains of peace, security and justice – rather than a state monopoly on legitimate physical force – prevail in most African societies.[160]

---

158 See Draft Report of KAIPTC and University of Queensland workshop on "Understanding and Working with Local Sources of Peace, Security and Justice in West Africa: National Stakeholders Workshop" Monrovia, Liberia, 29 June-1 July 2015.
159 Volker, Brown, Clements, (2009), op. cit.
160 Ibid

REGIONALLY ADAPTIVE HYBRIDITY AS A HOLISTIC, CONTEXT-SPECIFIC PEACEBUILDING FRAMEWORK?

In response to the conundrum of finding effective frameworks to the peacebuilding dilemma, several conceptual and empirical works have highlighted the multi-layered nature of socio-political disorder in conflict-affected settings.[161] This has culminated in a so-called 'local turn'[162] and the (re)emergence of concepts such as hybridity and adaptiveness[163] in the peacebuilding scholarship. This has resulted in an 'increasingly globalized literature on peacebuilding'[164] that deals with the encounter between the local and the international. In far too many cases, peacebuilding has been reduced to technical models based on checklists and templates to avoid politics. In some, peacebuilding becomes highly politicised, while lacking a common framework around which to mobilise competing interests and agendas.[165] To overcome these shortcomings, regionally adaptive hybridity in peacebuilding requires more systematic analysis and the mapping of conflict dynamics by both international and local actors. But it also requires credible platforms, institutions and mechanisms that can draw local and international actors around a common framework. As a result, I conflate two critical approaches to suggest an extra approach. I adapt de Coning's adaptive peacebuilding approach and Tschirgi's regional peacebuilding approach to discuss how a regionally adaptive hybrid approach can potentially create a framework and provide a flexible, sensitive response to context specificity that offers options for constant appraisal of the peacebuilding approach's goals

---

161   Boege et al., 'Building Peace and Political Community in Hybrid Political Orders'; Eric Scheye, 'Redeeming Statebuilding's Misconceptions: Power, Politics and Social Efficacy and Capital in Fragile and Conflict-Affected States', in Bryn W. Hughes, Charles T. Hunt, and Boris Kondoch. (Eds). Making Sense of Peace and Capacity-Building Operations: Rethinking Policing and Beyond, (Leiden: Martinus Nijhoff, 2010), 33–60; Bereketeab, Redie. 2020. 'Peacebuilding in Africa: Popular progressive versus neoliberal peacebuilding', in Adetula, V., Bereketeab, R., & Obi, C. (Eds.). (2020). Regional Economic Communities and Peacebuilding in Africa: Lessons from ECOWAS and IGAD (1st ed.). London: Routledge.

162   Johnson, 2022, et. al. p. 13; Mac Ginty, Roger and Richmond, O. P. 2013. 'The Local Turn in Peace Building: A Critical Agenda for Peace', Third World Quarterly, 34, (5), pp. 763–83.

163   de Coning, C. 2020. 'The six principles of Adaptive Peacebuilding', Conflict and Resilience Monitor, 2020/1, p.4.

164   McNamee and Muyangwa, op cit, p. 9.

165   Tschirgi, Necla. 2015. Bridging the Chasm between Domestic and International Approaches to Peacebuilding: Conceptual and Institutional Tools', Revista Crítica de Ciências Sociais, 7, (104).

– not merely countrywide, but also regionally and locally.[166] It is within this context that the UN and ECOWAS, for example, signed a Memorandum of Understanding (MoU) on 23 April 2018 to 'provide a framework and strengthen cooperation between the ECOWAS Commission and the UN Peacebuilding Support Office (PBSO) in support of peacebuilding and sustaining peace in West Africa, … strengthen coordination of efforts between the two entities and contribute to a more predictable and strategic partnership in the areas of conflict prevention, political dialogue, national reconciliation, democratic governance and human rights'.[167] Although this MoU has been signed, and the ideals of the partnership eloquently captured, the reality in the Sahel, which has become the 'underbelly of insecurity in Africa',[168] is that 'a truly regional approach to peacebuilding in the Sahel is still lacking, and regional cooperation – in areas such as security, conflict resolution and mediation, and political transition and governance – is fragmented'.[169] This results in the negative assessment that 'the current uncoordinated peacebuilding and peacekeeping in the Sahel is not working. There are too many actors pulling in too many directions.'[170] Although the UN, AU, EU and ECOWAS have sought to deepen 'their strategic partnership[s] … since 2017, collective peacebuilding efforts still lag behind cooperation in other areas. Different institutional mandates, policy frameworks and operational practices have led them to carve out distinct roles in the multilateral peacebuilding space, often impeding closer cooperation.'[171]

These partnership arrangements exist on paper; however, the mediation and peacebuilding processes that encourage the drivers of peace and limit the drivers of conflict at the local level are often ignored. The benefit of focusing on regionally adaptive hybrid peacebuilding and development is that it allows for a context-specific approach to tackling local issues that have an impact on local communities, but that could also have regional dimensions. While a key aspect of peacebuilding should be strengthening partnerships and local ownership, a critical fulcrum

166   Aning, K. 2014. 'Transnational threats and the challenges to peacekeeping in Mali', Conflict Trends, Vol. 14, No. 2, pp. pp. 11-17; Carey and Sen, op cit. p. 9.
167   UN and ECOWAS, 2018. Joint Communique on ECOWAS Commission and Peacebuilding Support Office, Memorandum of Understanding on Peacebuilding, at https://www.un.org/peacebuilding/sites/www.un.org.peacebuilding/files/documents/joint_press_statement_un-ecowas_mou_april_2018-final.pdf accessed 8 November 2022
168   United Nations, Security Council debate on peacebuilding. SC/15096, at Security Council Must Gain Early Political, Financial Support, Deepen Local Engagement, Draw in Women and Youth to Succeed in Peacebuilding | UN Press, 3 November 2022
169   Baudais, Virginie, Amal Bourhrous and Dylan O'Driscoll. 2021. Conflict Mediation and Peacebuilding in the Sahel: The Role of Maghreb Countries in an African Framework SIPRI Policy Paper 58, (Stockholm: SIPRI).
170   Ibid, p. 30; McCandless, (2019) p. 25; Adetula, et. al., p. 27.
171   Singh, P and Daniel Forti. 2020. 'Beyond 2020 Exploring the potential for a stronger UN-AU peacebuilding partnership', Africa Report, 28 | September at https://www.ipinst.org/wp-content/uploads/2020/09/AR-28-UN-AU-peacekeeping.pdf p. 1.

around which a regionally adaptive hybridity in peacebuilding investments is decided should not require local organisations to follow the priorities of international actors. Instead it should enable them to have the freedom to apply their local knowledge to meet the needs of local populations who oftentimes include actors beyond the formally recognised boundaries of the state.[172] Due to these shortcomings, de Coning argues for an approach that he terms 'adaptive peacebuilding';[173] it provides useful and applicable approaches to dealing and coping with complex crises in unstable societies.[174] As far as de Coning is concerned, adaptiveness comprises certain principles that can be used for coping with complexity in conflict resolution and peacebuilding. These principles can be summarised as follows:

- Actions taken to influence the sustainability of a specific peace process have to be context and time specific, and they have to emerge from a process that engages the societies themselves.
- It should be a participatory process that facilitates the emergence of a goal-oriented outcome. Variety is critical: as the outcome is uncertain, one must experiment with a variety of options across a spectrum of probabilities.
- Close attention should be paid to feedback, in order to determine which actions have a better effect. This requires an active participatory decision-making process that abandons those actions that perform poorly or that have negative side-effects; meanwhile, those that show more promise can be further adapted to introduce more variety, or can be scaled up to have greater impact.
- As an iterative process, assumptions should be reviewed and strategic planning adapted. The process is repeated continuously, because in highly complex contexts assessments are only relevant for a relatively short period before new dynamics come into play.[175]

Mali – which has been in the throes of ever-expanding regional violence since 2012 and has been subject to extensive international engagements – provides a useful example for testing how constructions of insecurity and the narratives of peacebuilding have manifested themselves within this space.

---

172 Part of this section draws on Baudais, Bourhrous and O'Driscoll, p. 32.
173 Cedric de Coning, Adaptive peacebuilding, International Affairs, Volume 94, Issue 2, March 2018, Pages 301–317.
174 Cedric de Coning. 2020. 'The six principles of Adaptive Peacebuilding', Conflict and Resilience Monitor, 2020/1, p.4.
175 Ibid.

THE SHIFT TO 'REGIONAL PEACEBUILDING'

Due to the conceptual fuzziness and wicked nature of the problems that peacebuilding seeks to deal with, Tschirgi has argued for a regionalised approach,[176] following on from Barry Buzan and Ole Waever's work on the inseparability of insecurities except when examined in a regional context.[177] 'Regional peacebuilding' is located within the continuously transforming field of new regionalism and the recognition of what has been termed the expansion of crises 'through the mobility of fighters and the proliferation of arms'.[178] According to Richard Kaplan: 'West Africa has acquired the image as a zone of poverty, high transaction costs, low civic participation, low resource allocation to the social sectors and political instability'[179]. With patterns of relationships characterised as 'new regionalism', West Africa is a region where the co-existence of multiple new and old actors are linked together in hybrid networks and coalitions that together are creating a wide range of complex regionalisation patterns.[180]

Others have described regional peacebuilding to include contemporary currents of transnational and cross-border flows – facilitated by geographical proximity – through wide ranging perspectives reflecting and affecting a complex interplay of local, regional and global forces simultaneously involving not only states, but also non-state, market and societal actors. For example, ECOWAS is a region that has established increasingly strong and binding relationships among states, to the extent that some form of cooperative civil societies have developed throughout the region and the regional institutions support such social interactions.[181]

The relevance of new regionalism to regional peacebuilding can also be traced where it has been used as a conceptual framework for analysing regional peace and security policies and plans. Conceived to be plural, multidimensional and involving

---

176   Tschirgi, N. 2002. 'Making the Case for a Regional Approach to Peacebuilding'. Journal of Peacebuilding & Development, 1(1), 25–38.

177   Buzan, Barry and Ole Waever, 2003. Regions and Powers: The Structure of International Society (Cambridge: Cambridge University Press), 40–82.

178   Adetula, et. al., op cit, p. 9; Aning, K. 2014. 'Transnational threats and the challenges to peacekeeping', Conflict Trends, Vol. 14, No. 2.

179   Kaplan, R. 1994. 'The Coming Anarchy: How scarcity, crime, overpopulation, tribalism, and disease are rapidly destroying the social fabric of our planet', The Atlantic Monthly, February Issue.

180   Söderbaum, Fredrik and J. A. Grant. 2003. The New Regionalism in Africa (London: Routledge); Bach, Daniel. 2013. 'Regionalism in Africa: concepts and context', in James Hentz, Ed., Routledge Handbook of African Security, Oxford: Routledge, pp.181ff.

181   ECOWAS and West Africa Civil Society Forum (WACSOF), West Africa Civil Society Initiative (WACSI), West Africa Police Commissioners Organisation (WAPCO),

governments and a variety of non-state actors, new regionalism (it is argued) results in a multiplicity of formal and informal regional governance structures and networks dealing with many issues. Critically, the questions that arise are: should all peacebuilding programming that crosses national borders be considered regional, or is something more required? If regional peacebuilding addresses structural causes of conflict across a region, does that mean that working on a key issue (e.g. governance) in multiple countries can be considered regional peacebuilding? Or would a regional programme require more – such as joint learning, and shared networks and platforms? Furthermore, when a peacebuilding programme targets or works with a regional organisation – for instance, a regional economic community – does that qualify the intervention as regional peacebuilding? Ettang, Maina and Razia seem to think so, as they define regional peacebuilding as: 'collective initiative[s] by various actors aimed at ensuring the absence of violent conflict and the presence of positive/sustainable peace from a regional perspective – considering the geographic and functional elements of the regional conflict complex ... with specific transnational issues that may not be in position to address'.[182] Considering the complexity of regional conflicts is an important aspect of the above definition. It emphasises that regional responses to conflicts that are regional or that have a regional dimension need to be informed by analysis that takes these dynamics into account. Beyond understanding regional dynamics is the need to analyse the complex local contexts that shape the regional conflict systems.

However, lack of consensus and clarity around what regional peacebuilding is or is not has implications for the shape and mode of interventions. Drawing from the above discussions, 'regional peacebuilding' is defined as 'peacebuilding that engages regionally to transform the regional conflict system in a way that promotes interlinkages between actors and draws from national and grassroots efforts and people across relevant countries and spheres, encompassing their participation'.[183] A critical part of this definition is that regional peacebuilding is informed by analysis of regional dynamics and related intricate local contexts through the lens of what Ettang, et. al. defines as the six key essentials of effective regional peacebuilding. It should: 1) engage regionally to transform the regional conflict system positively by targeting key drivers of the regional conflict; 2) undertake regional conflict analysis that should inform and shape responses, strategies and approaches sensitive to regional dynamics and related intricate local contexts in affected countries across the region; 3) promote interlinkages and collaboration between actors across the affected region, both horisontally and vertically; 4) draw on and engage with national, subnational and grassroots peacebuilding efforts across the affected region; 5) in-

---

182 'A Regional Approach to Peacebuilding – The Mano River Region', Policy & Practice Brief ISSUE # 006 May 2011; Adetula, op cit., p. 10.

183 Ibid.

volve the participation of affected peoples, including grassroots people, connecting them and building relationships across the affected region; and finally 6) embrace conflict-sensitivity as a core principle, by ensuring that the design, implementation and related processes – as well as the outcome of interventions – do not undermine peace or exacerbate conflict. These essentials are interlinked and underpin each other.

Though the jury is out on the regionalised adaptive hybrid approach to peacebuilding, the realities on the ground in Mali, Burkina Faso, Niger and the wider Sahel region point to veritable challenges and a need to reframe how peacebuilding is done. The argument has been made that, although '[a] number of African regional organisations, including the AU, ECOWAS and the G5 Sahel, are taking part in the Sahel peacebuilding processes ... their inclusiveness varies ... [and they] continue to struggle with finding the appropriate format for cooperation, one that integrates relevant parties instead of marginalizing them and driving them to pursue their agendas through other frameworks'.[184] This raises a fundamental question as to whether peacebuilding in the Sahel has become a wicked problem. If so, how can a regionalised understanding that understands and appreciates the complexity of stakeholders in Mali and the interlinkages to problems with its contiguous states (and even much further afield) be resolved?

---

184   Baudais, Virginie, Amal Bourhrous and Dylan O'Driscoll. 2021. Conflict Mediation and Peacebuilding in the Sahel: The Role of Maghreb Countries in an African Framework, SIPRI Policy Paper 58, (Stockholm: SIPRI).

After almost a decade of trial-and-error interventions, traditional authorities and others described in the UN Secretary-General's report as 'the vital forces of the nation' have now been invited to play key roles in the provision of peace, justice and security.

Page 53

Mberra, Mauritania, September 2016. Abel Ba, a community leader who together with his extended family fled his village of Nampalá, are among the 41,000 refugees from Mali living in the Mberra refugee camp. Photo: EU/ECHO/José Cendón.

CONCLUSION

I have argued in this paper that states can – and often do – develop in functional ways that may not necessarily follow a Weberian model. Therefore, promoting the Weberian idea of a modern state as the ultimate model of statehood is to ignore the contemporary realities and historical context of the emergence of the modern state in Africa. It is obvious from the foregoing discussions that many West African states in particular (but also African states generally) do not fit the description or criteria of the Weberian model of statehood. The authority to exercise legitimate force and the provision of peace, security and justice do not rest exclusively with state institutions. This is especially the case in fragile situations or in rural and semi-urban areas, where states are incapable of providing basic security and services. It is often the complex and interdependent relationships between both the modern and traditional states, characterised by a mix of conflict and (often) cooperation that explains state resilience.[185] Mali's present situation epitomises this. Furthermore, to fully appreciate these dynamics, post-conflict states must be substantially grounded in the socio-political circumstances, histories and relational networks of particular places.[186] Such an understanding moves beyond the received historiographies that shape and condition how states function. Thus, in Mali, we have seen how traditional authorities (involving religious and other community leaders) also play key roles in the provision of peace, justice and security.[187] After almost a decade of trial-and-error interventions, traditional authorities and others described in the UN Secretary-General's report as 'the vital forces of the nation'[188] have now been invited to play key roles in the provision of peace, justice and security. They continue to serve the needs of the majority of the people – especially in rural areas – showing the plurality of actors that communities rely on for the provision of security, peace and justice. The state, therefore, does not have a monopolistic position as the only agency providing peace, security, justice and other welfare services: it has to share authority, legitimacy and capacity with other institutions. There is, therefore, a need for recognition of the multiplicity of actors, in order to effectively combine elements of the Weberian model of governance and elements that stem from local indigenous traditions of governance. The question, therefore, is how to integrate the two systems more effectively, in order to better serve citizens in terms of service delivery, provision of peace, security and access to justice. It is important to search for new

---

185 African Security Sector Network. Hybrid Security Orders in Africa Concept paper.
186 See Aning and Brown, 2018. 'Introduction: Seeking peace in West Africa and the Pacific Island region – new directions' in Kwesi Aning, M. Anne Brown, Volker Boegge & Charles T. Hunt, (Eds) Exploring Peace formations: justice and security in post-conflict states. (London: Routledge).
187 UNSC. 2022. Situation in Mali Report of the Secretary-General, S/2022/731, 3 October.
188 Ibid p. 2.

ways of creating a mutual accommodation of state and traditional systems, in order to generate new forms of governance and so provide opportunities for peacebuilding and state-building.

As the Mali case shows, though it has been a regular element of contemporary peace and state-building endeavours, the application of international norms to the rebuilding of institutions – in this case the security institution – has not yielded the desired results. A bottom-up hybrid peace in Mali must fuse local structures, practices, values and identities that reflect the reality of the Malian experience; it must explore indigenous approaches to conflict resolution and localised responses to conflict. This calls for a bold effort at 'recentring' our understanding; the discourse surrounding the 'vernacular understandings and agency of people and groups'[189] on the margins implies neither that their agency is non-violent nor that it is non-exclusionary. It does not simply imply doing away with the state or renouncing its significance, but rather it underscores the importance of 'the complex array of forms of governance across populations, often articulating widespread social values, practices and ways of understanding the world; and, the nature of the interplay between state institutions (of whatever kind) and these forms of governance. It is in the character of this interaction that questions of participation, accountability and legitimacy are significantly located.'[190] To Tschirgi, hybrid peacebuilding must be a 'continually-negotiated political process ... that needs to be dynamic, conflict-sensitive and locally-grounded if it is to capture entrenched interests as well as changing realities in countries emerging from conflict'.[191] The crucial questions rather concern how to identify and reinforce those forms of local agency that build peace, fortify social justice and promote inclusive politics as 'strategic imperative'.[192] As has been argued elsewhere, investing in local and national capacities for peace are critical success factors. These factors – which span local and national resilience frameworks, improving and deepening adaptive capacities, strengthening social capital and social cohesion – are all significant for communities and societies as they respond to and endure shocks. Peacebuilding, therefore, 'has to develop better ways in which international, regional, national, and local peacebuilders can support and strengthen local and national capacities for peace, taking into account ... peace and security risks'.[193] This envisages a shift from the discourse that perceives 'the recipients of international efforts ... simply as sites of violence or dysfunction, rather than as also

---

189　Lind, Jeremy & Robin Luckham (2017) Introduction: security in the vernacular and peacebuilding at the margins; rethinking violence reduction, Peacebuilding, 5:2, p. 89-98.
190　Aning and Brown, 'Introduction'.
191　Tschirgi, 2015, p.81.
192　Newman, Edward. 2010. 'Peacebuilding as security in 'failing and conflict-prone' states', Journal of Intervention and Statebuilding, 4, (3), p.313.
193　See ACCORD-AU. 2020. 2020 Review of the United Nations Peacebuilding Architecture African Regional Consultation Report, 30 June 2020. p.7.

potentially generators of social order and relative peace'.[194] Such an approach will result in concrete responses to long-term violence, and at rebuilding societies from the concrete realities, relationships, histories and needs on the ground.[195]

194   Aning and Brown, 'Introduction'.
195   Ibid.

BIBLIOGRAPHY

ACCORD-AU. 2020. 2020 *Review of the United Nations Peacebuilding Architecture African Regional Consultation Report*, 30 June 2020. p. 7.

Abrahamsen, Rita. 2005. 'Blair's Africa: The Politics of Securitization and Fear', *Alternatives*, 30, pp. 55ff.

Adejumobi, Said. 2000. 'Elections in Africa: A fading Shadow of Democracy?' *International Political Science Review*, 21(1).

Adetula, V., Bereketeab, R., & Obi, C. (Eds.,).2020. *Regional Economic Communities and Peacebuilding in Africa: Lessons from ECOWAS and IGAD* (1st ed. London: Routledge. https://doi.org/10.4324/9781003093695).

Adu Boahen, Albert., 1966 *Topics in West African History*. London: Harlow.

Adu Boahen, J. F. Ade Ajayi, 1986. *Topics in West African History*, London: Longman Group.

Adu Boahen, Albert., Beiträgen von J., B Webster and M. Tidy, 1980. *The Revolutionary Years: West Africa since 1800*. London: Longman Group.

African Security Sector Network. Hybrid Security Orders in Africa Concept paper.

Ake, C. 1993. 'The Unique Case of African Democracy', *International Affairs* 69 (2), pp. 239–244.

Alison, Simon. 2012.'Military intervention in Mali: a dangerous idea with too much support', at https://www.theguardian.com/world/2012/oct/17/military-intervention-mali-dangerous-idea assessed 10 October 2022. Alison argues that, '…[to] be honest: it's not the humanitarian situation that is animating the international response, 17 October.

Andersen, Ben. 2015. 'What Kind of Thing is Resilience?' Politics, 35 (1), https://doi.org/10.1111/1467-9256.12079 pp. 60-66.

Aning, Kwesi. 2010. 'Security, war on terror and ODA', *Critical Studies on Terrorism*, 3 (2) pp. 7-26, https://doi.org/10.1080/17539151003594178.

Aning, K and A. Brown, 2018. 'Introduction: Seeking peace in West Africa and the Pacific Island region – new directions' in Kwesi Aning, M. Anne Brown, Volker Boegge & Charles T. Hunt, (Eds) *Exploring Peace formations: justice and security in post-conflict states*. (London: Routledge).

Aning, Kwesi et al. 2022. 'Decolonising Academic Collaboration: South-North Perspectives', *DIIS Policy Brief,* May https://pure.diis.dk/ws/files/5428162/DIIS_PB_Decolonising_Academic_Collaboration.pdf.

Aning, Kwesi. 2005. "The Challenges to Multilateral Interventions - UN, ECOWAS and Complex Political Emergencies in West Africa: A Critical Analysis', *Journal of Asian & African Studies*, 4, (1- 2).

Aning, K and E. Lartey. 2014. 'The role of RECs in peacebuilding in Africa: past experiences and the way forward' *Cairo Policy Briefs*, No. 3, November at https://www.cccpa-eg.org/publications-details/353.

Aning, Kwesi. M. Anne Brown, Volker Boege & Charles T. Hunt. 2018. *Exploring Peace formations: justice and security in post-conflict states* (London: Routledge).

Aning, K and L. Amedzrator. 2014.'Security in the Sahel: Linking the Atlantic to the Mediterranean', in Riccardo Alcaro and Nicoletta Pirozzi, (Eds) *Transatlantic Security from the Sahel to the Horn of Africa.*, (Rome: IAI Research Papers No. 12).

- 2014.'The Economics of Militancy and Islamist Extremism in the Sahel' in *Political stability and security in West and North Africa* (Toronto: World Watch: Expert Notes series publication No. 2014-04-01) at www.csis-scrs.gc.ca.

Aning, Kwesi, Fiifi Edu-Afful, 2016. 'African Agency in R2P: Interventions by African Union and ECOWAS in Mali, Cote D'ivoire, and Libya', *International Studies Review*, 18 (1), March, pp. 120–133, https://doi.org/10.1093/isr/viv017.

Aning, K. 2014. 'Transnational threats and the challenges to peacekeeping in Mali', *Conflict Trends*, Vol. 14, No. 2, pp. pp. 11-17.

Aning, K and Festus Aubyn. 2013. "Challenges in Mali: historic duty to ensure peace', *New Routes*, No. 2, (PDF).

Aning, Kwesi and Ilana Axelrod. 2020.'Mali, Democracy and ECOWAS's Sanctions Regime', *KAIPTC Policy Brief 9* | October 2020.

Annan, Kofi 1998. 'The Causes of Conflict and the Promotion of Durable Peace and Sustainable Development in Africa', Report of the Secretary-General to the Security Council, S/1998/318 (13 April, 1998), para. 63.

Aoi, Chiyuki, De Coning, Cedric, and Thakur, Ramesh Chandra, 2007. *Unintended Consequences of Peacekeeping Operations* (Tokyo and New York: United Nations University Press).

Archaya, Amitav, Paul Henri-Bischoff, Kwesi Aning, 2015. 'Africa in global international relations: emerging approaches to theory and practice – an introduction' in Amitav Archaya, Paul Henri-Bischoff, Kwesi Aning, Eds., *Africa in Global*

International Relations: emerging approaches to theory and practice (London: Routledge).

Arowosegbe. 2011. State reconstruction in Africa: the relevance of Claude Ake's political thought', *International Affairs*, 87 (3), May.

Aubyn, F. et al., 2019. 'UN Funding Cuts for Peacekeeping have Consequences for Ghana: After Sixty years of UN Peacekeeping' *DIIS Policy Brief*, https://www.diis.dk/en/research/un-funding-cuts-peacekeeping-consequences-ghana .

Aubyn, Festus. 2014, 'Policing and Peace Operations in Africa: Reflections On MINUSMA' unpublished paper.

Aubyn, F and Kwesi Aning. 2018. 'Challenging conventional understandings of statehood based on West African Realities' in Kwesi Aning, M. Anne Brown, Volker Boege & Charles T. Hunt. (Eds.), *Exploring Peace formations: justice and security in post-conflict states*. (London: Routledge).

Ba, Oumar. 2022. 'The Europeans and Americans Don't Know Africa': Of Translation, Interpretation, and Extraction', *Millennium- Journal of International Studies*, 50 (2), January, p. 550.

Ba, Boubacar and Morten Bøås (2013) *The Mali Presidential Elections: Outcomes and Challenges*, Oslo: Noref (Noref Report October 2013).

Bach, Daniel. 2013. 'Regionalism in Africa: concepts and context', in James Hentz, Ed., *Routledge Handbook of African Security*, Oxford: Routledge, pp.181ff.

Bagayoko, Niagale, Eboe Hutchful & Robin Luckham. 2016. 'Hybrid security governance in Africa: rethinking the foundations of security, justice and legitimate public authority', *Conflict, Security & Development*, 16:(1), pp. 1-32, DOI: 10.1080/14678802.2016.1136137.

Barnett, Michael., et al., 2007. 'Peacebuilding: What is in a name?', *Global Governance*, 13 (1), pp. 35-58, DOI:10.1163/19426720-01301004.

Bargués, Pol. 2020. 'Peacebuilding without peace? On how pragmatism complicates the practice of international intervention', *Review of International Studies*, 46 2).

Bargués-Pedreny, Pol & Xavier Mathieu 2018. 'Beyond Silence, Obstacle and Stigma: Revisiting the 'Problem' of Difference in Peacebuilding', *Journal of Intervention and Statebuilding*, 12 (3), pp. 283-299, https://doi.org/10.1080/1750 2977.2018.1513622.

Baudais, Virginie, Amal Bourhrous and Dylan O'Driscoll. 2021. Conflict Mediation and Peacebuilding in the Sahel: The Role of Maghreb Countries in an African Framework, *SIPRI Policy Paper* 58, (Stockholm: SIPRI).

Bennett, Karen. 2007. 'Epistemicide! The Tale of a Predatory Discourse', November, Translator 13(2):151-169.

Bereketeab, Redie. 2020. 'Peacebuilding in Africa: Popular progressive versus neoliberal peacebuilding', in Adetula, V., Bereketeab, R., & Obi, C. (Eds.). (2020). *Regional Economic Communities and Peacebuilding in Africa: Lessons from ECOWAS and IGAD* (1st ed.). London: Routledge. https://doi.org/10.4324/9781003093695.

Boeke, Sergei and Bart Schuurman. 2015. 'Operation Serval: the French Intervention in Mali', https://www.leidensecurityandglobalaffairs.nl/articles/operation-serval-the-french-intervention-in-mali.

Brauchler, Birgitte. 2017. 'Social engineering the local for peace', *Social Anthropology,* 25 (4), p. 437-453 https://doi.org/10.1111/1469-8676.12453.

Boas, Morten. 2013, 'Mali 2013: A Year of Elections and Further Challenges' http://www.e-ir.info/2013/12/22/mali-2013-a-year-of-elections-and-further-challenges.

Boege, Volker, Anne M. Brown, and Kevin P. Clements. (2009). 'Hybrid Political Orders, Not Fragile States'. *Peace Review,* 21(1), pp.13 -21. https://doi.org/10.1080/10402650802689997.

Boege, Volker, Anne Brown, Kevin Clements and Anna Nolan, *On Hybrid Political Orders and Emerging States: State Formation in the Context of 'Fragility',* http://www.berghof-foundation.org/fileadmin/redaktion/Publications/Handbook/Articles/boege_etal_handbook.pdf.

Volker, Boege, and Charles T Hunt. 2020. 'On 'travelling traditions': Emplaced security in Liberia and Vanuatu', *Cooperation and Conflict,* Vol. 55, Issue 4, Dec, pp. 498, https://doi.org/10.1177/0010836720954480.

Burke, Jason. 2022. 'International troops quit Mali as violence and Moscow's influence grow', https://www.theguardian.com/world/2022/nov/17/troops-quit-mali-violence-moscow-influence 17 November.

Buzan, Barry and Ole Waever, 2003. *Regions and Powers: The Structure of International Society* (Cambridge: Cambridge University Press), 40–82.

Carey, Henry F. and Onur Sen.2019. 'Bridging the Conceptual and Theoretical Divides on Peace and Peacebuilding', in Carey, H. (Ed.). (2020). *Peacebuilding Paradigms: The Impact of Theoretical Diversity on Implementing Sustainable Peace.* Cambridge: Cambridge University Press. doi:10.1017/9781108652162.

Charbonneau, B. 2021. 'Counter-insurgency governance in the Sahel', *International Affairs,* 97 (6), p. 1816.

Charbonneau, B. 2022. 'The climate of counterinsurgency and the future of security in the Sahel', *Environmental Science and Policy*, 138, https://doi.org/10.1016/j.envsci.2022.09.021.

Chinweizu, Ibekwe. 1987. *Decolonising the African mind* (Lagos: Sundoor).

Cold-Ravnkilde, S. M. and Katja Lindskov Jacobsen, 2020. 'Disentangling the security traffic jam in the Sahel: constitutive effects of contemporary interventionism', *International Affairs* 96 (4), 2020, p. 857.

Cooper, Frederick. 2001. 'What Is the Concept of Globalization Good for? An African Historian's Perspective', *African Affairs*, vol. 100, no. 399, pp. 189–213.

Cuc, Milan. "Mali on the Mend as Reforms Resume after Security Crisis", http://www.imf.org/external/pubs/ft/survey/so/2013/int123013a.htm.

Dalgaard-Nielsen, Anja. 2017. Organizational resilience in national security bureaucracies: Realistic and practicable? *Journal of Contingencies and Crises Management*, 25 (4), December, pp. 341-349, https://doi.org/10.1111/1468-5973.12164.

Davidson, Basil, F.K. Buah and J.F.A. Ajayi, 1977. *The Growth of African Civilization: A History of West Africa 1000-1800,* Longman Singapore Publishers.

de Coning, Cedric. 2020. 'The six principles of Adaptive Peacebuilding', *Conflict and Resilience Monitor*, 2020/1, p. 4.

de Coning, Cedric. Adaptive peacebuilding, *International Affairs*, Volume 94, Issue 2, March 2018, Pages 301–317, https://doi.org/10.1093/ia/iix251.

Devon DB, 'the Crisis in Mali: A Historical Perspective on the Tuareg People', *Global Research*, 1 February, 2013, http://www.globalresearch.ca/the-crisis-in-mali-a-historical-perspective-on-the-tuareg-people/5321407.

Dion, Ena and Joseph Sany. 2021. 'After Two Coups, Mali Needs Regional Support to Bolster Democracy Regional and international actors will need to prioritize locally devised and accepted solutions to tackle the roots causes of Mali's troubles', at https://www.usip.org/publications/2021/12/after-two-coups-mali-needs-regional-support-bolster-democracy 9 December.

Doyle, Michael W. and Nicholas Sambanis, 2000. 'International Peacebuilding: A Theoretical and Quantitative Analysis', *American Political Science Review* 94 (4), pp. 779-801.

Ekeh, Peter. 1975. "Colonialism and the Two Publics in Africa: A Theoretical Statement," *Comparative Studies in Society and History*, 17 (1).

Enloe, Cynthia, 1996. 'Margins, Silences and Bottom Rungs: How to Overcome the Underestimation of Power in the Study of International Relations', in Ken Booth, Steve Smith & Marysia Zalewski, Eds., *International Theory: Positivism and Beyond*. (Cambridge: Cambridge University Press), pp.186–202.

EU Training Mission Mali (EUTM Mali) at https://eutmmali.eu/wp-content/uploads/2022/01/20220113_Fact-Sheet-EUTM-sans-elections-22FEB_ENG.pdf.

European Diplomatic Academy, 2022. 'Opening remarks by High Representative Josep Borrell at the inauguration of the pilot programme', 13 October, at https://www.eeas.europa.eu/eeas/european-diplomatic-academy-opening-remarks-high-representative-josep-borrell-inauguration_en.

Falola, T. 1988 *Decolonizing African Studies: knowledge production, agency, and Voice* (Rochester, NY: University of Rochester Press).

Finlay, L. 1998. 'Reflexivity: an essential component for all research?', *British Journal of Occupational Therapy*, 61, (10): 453-456.

Forsyth, Miranda. et al. 2017. 'Hybridity in peacebuilding and development: a critical approach', *Third World Thematics*, 2 (4), p. 410.

Fuglestad, Finn. 1992. 'The Trevor-Roper trap or the imperialism of history: an essay', *History in Africa*, vol. 19, pp. 309–26.

Galtung, Johan 1976. 'Three Approaches to Peace: Peacekeeping, peacemaking and peacebuilding', in Johan Galtung, Ed., *Peace, War and Defence: Essays in Peace Research* (Copenhagen: Christian Ejlers).

Grovogui, Siba. N. (2002). Regimes of Sovereignty: International Morality and the African Condition. *European Journal of International Relations*, 8(3), 315–338. https://doi.org/10.1177/1354066102008003001.

Hounkpe, Mathias and Alioune, B. Gueye., '*The Role of Security Forces in the Electoral Process: The Case of Six West African Countries*' (Lagos: Friedrich-Ebert-Stiftung, 2010).

Hudson, Heidi. 2016. 'Decolonising gender and peacebuilding: feminist frontiers and border thinking in Africa', *Peacebuilding* 4 (2), pp.194ff https://doi.org/10.1080/21647259.2016.1192242.

Human Rights Watch, 'Mali: Islamist Armed Groups Spread Fear in North', http://www.hrw.org.

John Paul. 2012. 'The origins and evolution of infrastructures for peace', *Journal of Peacebuilding and Development*, 7 (3), https://doi.org/10.1080/15423166.2013.767604.

Johnson, A. K., Lechartre, J., Mart, Ş. G., Robison, M. D., & Hughes, C. 2023. Peace scholarship and the local turn: Hierarchies in the production of knowledge about peace. *Journal of Peace Research*, Vol. 60(4) 675–690 https://doi.org/10.1177/00223433221088035 p. 2.

Johnson, P. and Duberley, J. (2003) 'Reflexivity in management research', *Journal of Management Studies*, 40: 1279-1303.

Kaplan, R. 1994. 'The Coming Anarchy: How scarcity, crime, overpopulation, tribalism, and disease are rapidly destroying the social fabric of our planet', *The Atlantic Monthly*, February Issue.

Keita, Khalifa. 'Conflict and Conflict Resolution in the Sahel: The Tuareg Insurgency in Mali,' *Small Wars & Insurgencies* 9, no. 3 (1998);

Lara, Christian and Bariel Delsol. 2020. *Sustaining Peace in Burkina Faso: Responding to an Emerging Crisis.* New York: International Peace Institute, May.

Levin, K. B., Cashore, S. Bernstein, & Auld, G. (2012). Overcoming the tragedy of super wicked problems: Constraining our future selves to ameliorate global climate change. *Policy Sciences*, 45, pp. 121–152. DOI 10.1007/s11077-012-9151-0.

Lind, Jeremy & Robin Luckham (2017) Introduction: security in the vernacular and peacebuilding at the margins; rethinking violence reduction, *Peacebuilding*, 5:2, 89-98, doi:10.1080/21647259.2016.1277008.

'Mali: Security situation deteriorates, human rights concerns rise', at https://news.un.org/en/story/2022/08/1124692.

Mamdani, M. 1996. *Citizen and Subject: Contemporary Africa and the Legacy of Late Colonialism* (Princeton: Princeton University Press), p. 9.

Maru, Mehari T. 2013, 'AFISMA: Military ahead of Politics http://studies.aljazeera.net/en/reports/2013/02/20132148940690455 , [accessed 3 October 2022].

Mateos, Òscar, & Rodríguez, A. I. 2022. Understanding Peace, Conflict and Security Through Alternative Narratives. *Tripodos*, (51).

McCandless, E. (2021). 'Critical Evolutions in the Peacebuilding-Development Praxis Nexus: Crisis and Complexity, Synergy and Transformation'. *Journal of Peacebuilding & Development*, 16(2), https://doi.org/10.1177/15423166211017832.

McCandless, E. 2019. 'Beyond Liberal and Local Peacebuilding Three Critical Framings to Approach the Complexity of Conflict and Fragility in Africa', *Africa Insight*, 49.

McGinty, Roger and Richmond, O. P. 2013. 'The Local Turn in Peace Building: A Critical Agenda for Peace', *Third World Quarterly*, 34, (5), pp. 763–83.

McNamee, Terence and Monde Muyangwa2021. *The State of Peacebuilding in Africa: Lessons Learned for Policymakers and Practitioners.* (Cham: Palgrave Macmillan).

Meagher, K. (2012), 'The Strength of Weak States? Non-State Security Forces and Hybrid Governance in Africa'. *Development and Change*, 43, p. 1074. https://doi.org/10.1111/j.1467-7660.2012.01794.

Mudimbe, V. Y. *The Invention of Africa*, (Bloomington, IN: Indiana University Press).

Nadarajah, Suthaharan and Rampton, David, 2015. 'The limits of hybridity and the crisis of liberal peace', *Review of International Studies*, 41 (1) pp. 49–72.

Newman, E. 2011. 'A human security peace-building agenda', *Third World Quarterly* 32, (10), pp 1737–1756.

Newman, Edward. 2010. 'Peacebuilding as Security in 'Failing' and Conflict Prone States', *Journal of Intervention and Statebuilding*, 4 (30, 305-322, DOI: 10.1080/17502977.2010.498935.

Newman, Edward 2013. The violence of statebuilding in historical perspective: implications for peacebuilding, *Peacebuilding*, 1 (1), pp. 141-157, DOI: 10.1080/21647259.2013.756281.

Nossiter, Adam. 'Soldiers Overthrow Mali Government in Setback for Democracy in Africa' http://www.nytimes.com/2012/03/23/world/africa/mali-coup-france-calls-for-elections.html?pagewanted=all&_r=0.

Nossiter, Adam and Peter Tinti, 2013, 'Mali Holds Elections After Year of Turmoil' http://www.nytimes.com/2013/07/29/world/africa/mali-holds-elections-after-year-of-turmoil.html.

Olonisakin, Funmi, Alagaw Ababu Kifle & Alfred Muteru (2021) Introduction: reframing narratives of peace-building and state-building in *Africa, Conflict, Security & Development,* 21 (4), pp.401ff, DOI: 10.1080/14678802.2021.1974700.

Omeje, K., (ed.), 2018. 'Introduction'. In Peacebuilding in Contemporary Africa: In *Search of Alternative Strategies*. London, New York: Routledge, 3–19.

Osaghae, E.E. 2006. Colonialism and Civil Society in Africa: The Perspective of Ekeh's Two Publics. *Voluntas* 17, 233–245. https://doi.org/10.1007/s11266-006-9014-4.

Paris, R 2002. 'International peacebuilding and the 'mission civilisatrice', *Review of International Studies* 28, p. 638.

Paffenholz, Thania. 2015. 'Unpacking the Local Turn in Peacebuilding: a critical assessment towards an agenda for future research'. *Third World Quarterly* 36 (5) pp.857-874 https://doi.org/10.1080/01436597.2015.1029908.

Peters, B Guy. 2017. 'What is so wicked about wicked problems? A conceptual analysis and a research program, *Policy and Society,* 36 (3), September, pp. 385–396, https://doi.org/10.1080/14494035.2017.1361633.

Powell, Nathaniel. 2022. 'Why France failed in Mali', https://warontherocks. com/2022/02/why-france-failed-in-mali/ February 21, accessed 17.11.22.

Pugh, Michael. 2004. 'Peacekeeping and critical theory', *International Peacekeeping* 11 (1), p. 48, https://doi.org/10.1080/1353331042000228445.

Richmond, O.P. 2008. *Peace in International Relations* (London: Routledge).

Richmond, O. 2009. 'The Romanticisation of the Local: Welfare, Culture and Peacebuilding', *The International Spectator,* 44 (1) pp.149ff March, DOI:10.1080/03932720802693044.

Richmond, O.P. 2011 'De-romanticizing the local, de-mystifying the international: hybridity in Timor Leste and the Solomon Islands', *The Pacific Review,* 24 (1) pp. 115-136, DOI: 10.1080/09512748.2010.546873.

Richmond, O.P. 2013. 'Peace formation and local infrastructures for peace', *Alternatives: Global, Local, Political,* 38 (4), pp. 271-287.

Schwikowski, Martina. 2022. 'Europe's troop withdrawal leaves Mali in limbo', https://www.dw.com/en/europes-troop-withdrawal-leaves-mali-in-limbo/a-60817940 17 February.

Scheye, Eric., 'Redeeming Statebuilding's Misconceptions: Power, Politics and Social Efficacy and Capital in Fragile and Conflict-Affected States', 2010. in Bryn W. Hughes, Charles T. Hunt, and Boris Kondoch. (Eds). *Making Sense of Peace and Capacity-Building Operations: Rethinking Policing and Beyond,* (Leiden: Martinus Nijhoff, 2010), pp.33–60.

Shurkin, Michael. 2014. France's War in Mali - Lessons for an Expeditionary Army. https://www.rand.org/pubs/research_reports/RR770.html.

Singh, P and Daniel Forti. 2020. 'Beyond 2020 Exploring the potential for a stronger UN-AU peacebuilding partnership', *Africa Report,* 28 | September at https://www.ipinst.org/wp-content/uploads/2020/09/AR-28-UN-AU-peacekeeping.pdf p. 1.

Stewart, Dona, J. *What is next for Mali? The Roots of Conflict and Challenges to Stability.* Washington: Strategic Studies Institute and U.S. Army War College Press, 2013.

Söderbaum, Fredrik and J. A. Grant. 2003. *The New Regionalism in Africa* (London: Routledge).

Tieku, Thomas Kwasi, 2021. 'The Legon School of International Relations', *Review of International Studies,* 47(5) pp. 656-671. doi:10.1017/S0260210521000395.

Trevor-Roper, Hugh. 1966. *The rise of Christian Europe* (London: Thames & Hudson).

Tschirgi, N. 2003. *Peacebuilding as the Link between Security and Development: Is the Window of Opportunity Closing?* (New York: International Peace Academy).

Tschirgi, N. 2002. 'Making the Case for a Regional Approach to Peacebuilding'. *Journal of Peacebuilding & Development,* 1(1), 25–38. https://doi.org/10.1080/15 423166.2002.568389302629.

Tschirgi, Necla. 2015. Bridging the Chasm between Domestic and International Approaches to Peacebuilding: Conceptual and Institutional Tools', *Revista Crítica de Ciências Sociais,* 7, (104) DOI:10.4000/RCCSAR.605.

Tull, D.M. 2019. 'Rebuilding Mali's army: the dissonant relationship between Mali and its international partners', *International Affairs* 95 (2) pp. 405–22.

UNSC, Situation in Mali: report of the Secretary-General, UN Doc. S/2021/519 (New York, 1 June 2021) UN Secretary-General's reports on Mali, present a dire picture in which the situation has steadily deteriorated since 2015. 'The security situation in the Sahel subregion continued to deteriorate.'

UN General Assembly and Security Council, Peacebuilding and Sustaining Peace—Report of the Secretary-General, UN Doc. A/72/707–S/2018/43, January 18, 2018.

UNSC, 2014, Report of the Secretary-General on Children and Armed Conflict in Mali, /2014/267/, 14 April 2014. New York: United Nations.

UN/ECOWAS MoU on Peacebuilding.

UNSC. 2022. Report of the Secretary-General on the situation in Mali (S/2022/731), 3 October.

UN and ECOWAS, 2018. Joint Communique on ECOWAS Commission and Peacebuilding Support Office, Memorandum of Understanding on Peacebuilding, at https://www.un.org/peacebuilding/sites/www.un.org. peacebuilding/files/documents/joint_press_statement_un-ecowas_mou_ april_2018-final.pdf accessed 8 November 2022.

United Nations, Security Council debate on peacebuilding. SC/15096, at Security Council Must Gain Early Political, Financial Support, Deepen Local

Engagement, Draw in Women and Youth to Succeed in Peacebuilding | UN Press, 3 November 2022.

UNSC. 2022. Situation in Mali Report of the Secretary-General, S/2022/731, 3 October.

UN, 1992. *An agenda for peace : preventive diplomacy, peacemaking and peace-keeping : report of the Secretary-General* pursuant to the statement adopted by the Summit Meeting of the Security Council on 31 January.

United Nations (UN), 'Transforming our World: the 2030 Agenda for Sustainable Development' (United Nations General Assembly, 2015).

UN, 'The Challenge of Sustaining Peace: Report of the Advisory Group of Experts for the 2015 Review of the United Nations Peacebuilding Architecture' (New York: United Nations, 2015), pp. 7, 8, 18.

UN, 'Peacebuilding and Sustaining Peace: Report of the Secretary-General' (General Assembly and Security Council, 2018), p. 1.

UN Security Council Authorizes Deployment of African-Led International Support Mission in Mali for Initial Year-Long Period, 20 December 2012 Security Council SC/10870 at https://press.un.org/en/2012/sc10870.doc.htm.

van Ostaeyen, Pieter and Kwesi Aning, 2023. 'Status of ISWAP and ISGS in West Africa and Sahel', at CEP-KAS_Paper 2_Status of ISWAP and ISGS in West Africa and Sahel,_June 2023.pdf (counterextremism.com).

Vijay Prashad. 2022. Africa Does Not Want to Be a Breeding Ground for the New Cold War: The Forty-Fourth Newsletter.

Vijay Prashad. 2022. 'Africa Doesn't Want to Be a New-Cold-War Breeding Ground' — Strategic Culture (strategic-culture.org).

wa Thiong'o, Ngũgĩ . 1986. *Decolonising the mind: the politics of language in African literature* (London and Portsmouth, NH: James Currey and Heinemann, 1986).

Wai, Zubairu. 2022. 'About a Will to Power: Post-cold War Conflicts and the Politics of Knowledge Production', *Tripodos*, number 51, p.34 https://doi.org/10.51698/tripodos.

WANEP, 'MALI: Managing the Damage of a Complex' http://www.wanep.org, [accessed 3 October 2012].

Williams, P. 2021. 'Learning lessons from peace operations in Africa', in McNamee, T and M. Muyangwa (Eds.), *The State of Peacebuilding in Africa: Lessons Learned for Policymakers and Practitioners*, (Cham: Palgrave Macmillan), pp. 15-32.

Wilén, Nina and Paul D. Williams. 2022. 'What Are the International Military Options for the Sahel?', at https://theglobalobservatory.org/2022/04/what-are-the-international-military-options-for-the-sahel.

Woodward, S.L. 2017. *The Ideology of Failed States. Why Intervention Fails* Cambridge: Cambridge University Press.

World Bank, "The Malian Economy Holds Steady in the Face of Crisis" http://www.worldbank.org/en/news/feature/2013/03/14/the-malian-economy-holds-steady-in-the-face-of-crisis.

Zaum, Dominik, 2011. 'Review essay; beyond the "Liberal Peace', *Global Governance: A Review of Multilateralism and International Organizations*, 18 (1), pp. 121-132. https://doi.org/10.1163/19426720-01801010.

THE CLAUDE AKE MEMORIAL PAPERS SERIES

The Claude Ake Visiting Chair, set up in 2003 by the Department of Peace and Conflict Research, Uppsala University (DPCR) and the Nordic Africa Institute (NAI) with funding from the Swedish government and Uppsala University, honours the memory of Professor Claude Ake (1939-1996), a Nigerian political scientist. It is intended for scholars who, like him, combine a profound commitment to scholarship with a strong advocacy for social justice. Based on the research, they pursue while in Uppsala, the holders of the Claude Ake Visiting Chair give a public lecture, which, in a general sense, relates to the work of Claude Ake. The lecture is based on a paper that is subsequently published jointly by DPCR and NAI in the Claude Ake Memorial Papers (CAMP) series. Below is a list of previous titles in the series:

1. JINADU, L. Adele; Explaining and Managing Ethnic Conflict in Africa: Towards a Cultural Theory of Democracy (2007).

2. OBI, Cyril I.; No Choice, But Democracy: Prising the People out of Politics in Africa? (2008).

3. SESAY, Amadu; The African Union: Forward March or About Face-Turn? (2008).

4. BOAFO-ARTHUR, Kwame; Democracy and Stability in West Africa: The Ghanaian Experience (2008).

5. VILLA-VICENCIO, Charles; Where the Old Meets the New: Transitional Justice, Peacebuilding and Traditional Reconciliation Practices in Africa (2009).

6. MOHAMED, Adam Azzain; Evaluating the Darfur Peace Agreement: A Call for an Alternative Approach to Crisis Management (2009).

7. MBABAZI, Pamela K; The Oil Industry in Uganda: A Blessing in Disguise or an all Too Familiar Curse? (2013).

8. ADETULA, Victor A.O.; African Conflicts, Development and Regional Organisations in the Post-Cold War International System (2015).

9. GOBODO-MADIKIZELA, Pumla; What Does It Mean to be Human in the Aftermath of Historical Trauma? Re-envisioning The Sunflower and Why Hannah Arendt was Wrong (2016).

10. MURITHI, Tim; Regional Reconciliation in Africa: The Elusive Dimension of Peace and Security (2019).

11. HUDSON, Heidi, A (Wo)man for all seasons: Amos Tutuola and the Gendering of Peace in Africa (2019).

12. OSAGHAE, Eghosa E. Federal Solutions to State Failure in Africa (2020).

All titles can be downloaded in full text at the NAI web site www.nai.uu.se.